SAYINGS OF THE AYATOLLAH KHOMEINI:

Political, Philosophical, Social, and Religious

Extracts from three major works by the Ayatollah:
Valayate-Faghih (The Kingdom of the Learned)
Kashfol-Asrar (The Key to Mysteries)
Towzihol-Masael (The Explanation of Problems)

Selected and translated from the Persian by Jean-Marie Xaviere with preface and explanatory notes.

English edition translated by Harold J. Salemson and specially edited by Tony Hendra.

Special introduction by Clive Irving.

SAYINGS OF THE AYATOLLAH KHOMEINI:
POLITICAL, PHILOSOPHICAL, SOCIAL, AND RELIGIOUS
*A Bantam Book/published by arrangement with
Editions Libres-Hallier*

PRINTING HISTORY

Published in France as Principes de l'Ayatollah Khomeiny:
Philosophiques, Sociaux & Religieux. *Copyright © 1979 by
Editions Libres-Hallier.*

Published in Brazil as Principios Politicos Filosoficos, Socias e
Religiosos. *Copyright © 1979 by Editions Libres-Hallier.*

Bantam edition/March 1980

ISBN 0-553-14032-9

Published simultaneously in the United States and Canada

Bantam Books are published by Bantam Books, Inc. Its trademark, consisting of the words "Bantam Books" and the por-
trayal of a bantam, is Registered in U.S. Patent and Trademark
Office and in other countries. Marca Registrada. Bantam
Books, Inc., 666 Fifth Avenue, New York, New York 10019.

PRINTED IN THE UNITED STATES OF AMERICA

0 9 8 7 6 5 4 3 2 1

PUBLISHER'S NOTE

SAYINGS OF THE AYATOLLAH KHOMEINI: POLITICAL, PHILOSOPHICAL, SOCIAL AND RELIGIOUS presents excerpts from the religious teachings of one of the most controversial leaders of our time. Based on the original French compilation, LES PRINCIPES DE L'AYATOLLAH KHOMEINY (Editions Libres-Hallier; September, 1979), it draws upon three major treatises by the Ayatollah, published in Persian over his sixteen years of exile: KINGDOM OF THE LEARNED (Valayate-Faghih), THE KEY TO MYSTERIES (Kashfol-Asrar), and THE EXPLANATION OF PROBLEMS (Towzihol-Masael). This body of work was largely derived from the lectures and speeches of the Ayatollah to his students. It prescribes a rigorous and comprehensive code of behavior, which is upheld by his followers as holy law.

Since its original publication in France, SAYINGS OF THE AYATOLLAH KHOMEINI has aroused interest worldwide. The American press has widely reported its existence and quoted liberally from its startling contents. Now for the first time, what has become known as "the little green book" of the Ayatollah Khomeini is available to the English-speaking public in book form. Here are the Iranian patriarch's maxims on everything from personal hygiene to divine revelation.

SAYINGS OF THE AYATOLLAH KHOMEINI provides insights into the mind of a man whose actions have shaken the world. It should be read by anyone who wishes to gain a deeper understanding of the current Iranian crisis and its impact on America and on the world.

Contents

Special Introduction by Clive Irving   vi
Editor's Note   xi
Preface   xiii

PART I POLITICAL AND PHILOSOPHICAL SAYINGS

1 Islam as a Revolutionary Religion   3
2 Islam and Colonialism   7
3 The Islamic Republic   15
4 The Rule of the Clergy   22
5 The Imam   25
6 Islamic Justice   28
7 Youth   32
8 Media and Propaganda   35

PART II SOCIAL AND RELIGIOUS SAYINGS

9 On the Manner of Urinating and Defecating   39
10 On the Manner of Eating and Drinking   44
11 On Purity and Impurity   48
12 On Purification   56
13 On the Nature of Water   65
14 On Ablution   69
15 On the Five Namaz   76
16 On Prayers in Case of Natural Phenomena   81
17 On Fasting   83
18 On Woman and Her Periods   88
19 On Marriage, Adultery, and Congugal Relations   94
20 On Divorce   111
21 On the Mortuary Ritual   115
22 On Finance and Taxes   118
Addenda   123

Special Introduction

To anyone reared and educated into the assumptions of western life, these are words from an alien mind. Many of the sentiments expressed here will seem—by turns—offensive, risible, pathological, obsessive. But their strangeness cannot be lightly cast aside. They must be explained and judged not by the standards of our world, but by that of the Ayatollah, their author. For these are the words of a man who brought down—with words not arms—the most elaborately armed regime in the Islamic world.

Ayatollah Ruhollah Khomeini is a phenomenon of the Islamic world and he has unsettled that world as much as our own. But the fact that he is an Iranian counts as much as the fact that he is a Muslim. For centuries Iran—or, as it then was, Persia—has given its own peculiar flavor to Islam. Khomeini is the most potent embodiment of the Iranian strain of Islam since the 16th century.

The first thing to understand of Khomeini is that he is not an Arab. The Arabs established Islam as a world religion with astonishing speed. Within a century they had carried its word as far as central France in the west and into the heart of Asia in the east. Their first wave out of the Arabian Peninsula engulfed Persia in the middle of the seventh century AD. The Arabs humiliated in battle what had been once the most feared army of the Orient, the only army to check the Roman Empire in the east. Persia became just one of numerous subject colonies of the Islamic empire, and its old religion of Zoroastrianism retreated into enclaves.

The psychological damage of this defeat to the Persian nature was permanent. The recovery of Persian self-esteem became linked to a belief that Islam was enhanced by its exposure to Persian culture. In truth, it was— in sublime religious architecture, calligraphy and poetry. But more than a cultural influence was needed; there had to be a stronger theological distinction between the Arab and the Persian.

It came at the beginning of the 16th century. A 14-year-old "messiah" appeared at the head of a band of murderous Turkoman tribesmen and rode into Persia. His name was Ismail and he preached through fiery poetry the cause of a minority Islamic sect, the Shi'ites. "I am God's mystery," he announced, and in a pitiless *jihad*, or holy war, he snatched control of Persia and enforced Shi'a Islam as the national religion. The adoption of Shi'ism enabled Persians to proclaim their piety as Muslims and at the same time to stand apart from the predominantly Sunni Arabs.

The division between Sunni and Shi'a arose from an early feud over who were the legitimate successors of the prophet Mohammed. Mohammed's cousin and son-in-law Ali, and subsequently Ali's second son Husein, were both killed in disputes over the succession. Their Sunni opponents prevailed but the martyrdoms of Ali and Husein created a powerful legend that reaches to the heart of Khomeini's own attraction.

Fused with Persian nationalism, the clarity of a new religious identity was a unifying force in a land barely a nation at all, containing (as it still does) many divisions—ethnic, tribal, economic and social. But this concentration of allegiance also contained the seeds of an enduring conflict—between the secular and religious authorities for the ultimate control of the state. Some Shahs were clever enough to advertise their piety and compromise with the clergy; others offended the faithful with grandiosity and decadent living. When the country was plundered by venal monarchs the only enduring loyalty of the people was to the religion. And when, after two centuries of relentless decay, a new dynasty devoted itself to modernizing Persia its most determined opponents were the clergy.

The Pahlavi dynasty, initiated by an army general and inherited by his son, Mohammed Reza Pahlavi, was in the end not equal to the galvanic appeal of the new "savage messiah," Ayatollah Ruhollah Khomeini. At a decisive moment Khomeini provided the historical alternative to secular misrule. He sloganized a deep resistance to western values and utilized a crude xenophobia against the U. S. and Zionism in particular. But he also unleashed something from the heart of the Iranian character, the appeal of martyrdom. "Our only basis of reference," he said of his revolution, "is the time of the prophet and Imam Ali." To a Shi'ite, and especially to an Iranian Shi'ite, death in the tradition of Ali and Husein not only ensures sanctity but it also satisfies the tragic folk memory of Persian history—the land overrun and exploited by aliens, ransacked and defiled, but always resurgent. Khomeini has shown an instinctive grasp of this psyche. Yet, ironically, his own Iranian roots are fragile.

Khomeini's grandfather was born in Kashmir. Khomeini's father was born after the family moved west into Iran. Khomeini must appreciate the paradox that the dynasty he brought down was probably more purely Persian in its bloodline than any for centuries.

For all Muslims, Sunni and Shi'a, the only infallible word of God is the Koran, revealed to the prophet Mohammed by the Angel Gabriel. The word "Islam" means "submission,"submission to the single authority of God. Unlike Christianity, Islam has no ordained hierarchy and the Muslim communicates directly with his God, who is never tangible. Within Shi'a Islam theological learning and authority are in the hands of the ayatollahs, whose number is not fixed, who are not formally elected and who "emerge" by the consent of their peers. Khomeini owes his singular status not to being a profound theologian but to his successful fusion of theology and politics. The zeal of his followers has transgressed at least one of the Koranic taboos: idolatry. The flagrant use of his image and the open use of the title "imam" are blasphemous to many Muslims. With the exit of the Shah, Iran seemed to need one icon to replace another.

The Koran offers a comprehensive and comprehensible code for living. It removes the caprice and whim of kingly laws. It provides not only spiritual inspiration but detailed guidance for the minutae of everyday living, especially for family relationships. It is here where the emancipated western eye begins to balk. Male primacy is inherent in the Koranic code. It was the Shah's attempt to emancipate women that provoked some of the most violent reactions from the clergy. The edicts of the Ayatollah, as revealed here, add up to a way of life that is inimical to almost everything the Shah prescribed.

The most aberrant note in Khomeini's creed is not the Islamic fundamentalism, which is to be seen in many places outside Iran, but its vengefulness. His loathing of the Pahlavi dynasty became remorseless and personalized; even the lightest association with that regime invited summary retribution. Unbalanced by this spirit, Khomeini sabotaged his own revolution. If the Iranians had taken their legitimate grievances to the right forum they would have kept the moral advantage with which they began their revolution. Instead, this advantage was forfeited by their own lawlessness. As to why this tragic error was made, these texts are of help. They are not just alien but alienating. They reveal one man's state of mind. They do not, however, reveal more. A faith outlives its interpreters.

CLIVE IRVING

Editor's Note

This edition of what has come to be known internationally as "the Little Green Book of the Ayatollah Khomeini" is based lagely on the original French compilation, *Les Principes Politiques, Philosophiques, Sociaux et Religieux de L'Ayatollah Khomeiny,* which was originally published by Editions Libres-Hallier in 1979.

Special care has been taken to present a responsible translation of the Ayatollah's sayings; everything here has been checked against the original Persian sources for accuracy. The general organization of the material follows the French edition wherever possible. Furthermore, we have supplemented the first section of the book, on the Ayatollah's political beliefs, with selections from Khomeini's major political treatise, the "Valayate Faghih."

A peculiarly untranslatable phrase, "Valayate Faghih" could be rendered as "Kingdom of the Learned," by which "The Rule of The Clergy" is implied. That the holy men of Islam, and in particular the Imam, or leader, are the sole political and judicial arbiters of the affairs of state is fundamental to Khomeini's thinking, to his vision of Iran's future, and to his own role in that future. Concurrent with that belief is the comprehensive scope of Islamic dictates, which prescribe every conceivable aspect of daily life, from personal hygiene to divine revelation.

Khomeini's writings cannot be viewed as representative of Islam. As leader of the Shi'ite branch of Islam, Khomeini speaks for a minority of the world's Moslem population. And as the self-styled messenger of the Prophet Mohammed, the Ayatollah follows in a long line of imams, or messiahs, who have interpreted the Koran in their own manner.

With this English language edition of "the Little Green Book," we can perhaps begin to educate ourselves about a mind set we must understand in order to deal with seemingly incomprehensible events. Perhaps we may be better able to deal with a world in which the modern and the medieval clash so dramatically.

TONY HENDRA

Preface

Iran has recently been the scene of one of the most overwhelming political and social upheavals of our time: an upheaval which overthrew one of the oldest monarchies in the world and transformed imperial Iran into a republic, something unprecedented in the three-thousand-year history of that country. However, it is not a republic like any other, but a "fundamentalist Islamic republic" in the strictest sense of that term, which in the eyes of those at its helm makes it different from all other republics in the world, as well as from all other Moslem republics.

This first "fundamentalist Islamic republic" in the whole history of Islam is at present represented by a chief who dominates it ideologically, politically, socially, spiritually, and religiously.

His authority allows of no dissent or controversy, since according to him it is dictated by divine right. The name of this chief is, of course, the Ayatollah Khomeini, a name that has perhaps been heard more often than any other in recent months.

We may assume that Khomeini's Iran will to a large extent reshape many of the accepted political, strategic, economic, and social facts of today's world, not only because of the country's geographical position and its immense petroleum wealth, but also because of the echo its "Islamic" revolution has found throughout the Moslem world, where nostalgic voices have been raised in favor of similar revolutions.

Therefore, it is to everyone's interest to know the principles and laws of this newborn Islamic republic which is the object of increasing curiosity in the West; for is not this very West the number one target of the new leaders of Iran and especially of Iran's paramount chief, who systematically refers to it in his speeches, writings, and theological teachings as being decadent, rotten, corrupt, tyrannical, imperialistic, and anti-Islamic?

Let us look then at the principles and laws that the Patriarch proclaims to be the only truths.

The "Khomeini doctrine" traces these truths to a divine origin and maintains that the laws based upon them will for all time rule all of humanity. According to this doctrine, they were revealed fourteen centuries ago to all mortal beings by the Prophet of God, Mohammed, son of Abdullah, whose Message abolished all previous truths, including those revealed by all other prophets. They are crystallized in the eternal laws emanating from Almighty God, which are subject to no alteration, but must be implicitly obeyed and rigorously applied.

The "civil code" of these laws, of course, is the Koran. But in order for mankind to understand and apply it, they need the interpretation and commentaries made of the Koran by the Twelve Imams who were direct descendants of the Prophet,* and in the days since the disappearance of the Twelfth Imam,† by those who represent him on earth.

In Iran today, it is the Ayatollah Khomeini who claims to be fulfilling this sacred mission. This explains why death sentences have been pronounced by "Islamic tribunals" against those indicted for having struggled against God on earth, against the Twelfth Imam, and his *nayeb* (deputy or locum tenens), in this case, of course, the Ayatollah.

The present book, a group of selections from three of the major works of the Ayatollah Khomeini, includes such passages as seem to serve the needs of the day. The original texts, in the Persian language, run to 263, 334, and 639 pages respectively, and have had printings in the tens of thousands. Full or partial reproduction of them as well as their translation is free to any who choose to do so, in order that they may gain greater currency and thus encourage the spread of the Moslem faith.

---

*According to Shi'ite tradition; Sunni Moslems do not believe in the Twelve Imams.

†In Shi'ite doctrine, the Twelfth Imam, alive but hidden somewhere among mankind, will make himself known again to bring an era of universal justice and true faith on earth.

The first work is entitled *Kashef-of-Gheta* or *Valayaté-Faghih* (The Kingdom of the Learned); the second is *Kashfol-Asrar* (The Key to Mysteries); and the third is *Towzihol-Masaël* (The Explanation of Problems).

Their publisher describes the author as "the Valiant Warrior, Paramount Chief, Sublime Guide, Moses of our time, Smasher of idols, Exterminator of tyrants, Liberator of humanity, His Holiness the Ayatollah Supreme Imam Ruhollah Mussavi Khomeini—May our souls be submissive to him."

In *The Realm of the Learned* and *The Key to Mysteries,* the Ayatollah Khomeini sets forth his political and philosophical principles concerning Islamic governments, the Moslem world, international politics, justice and Koranic laws, subversive activities, and so on. In *The Explanation of Problems,* he is writing not as a politician, but rather as the Patriarch of the Shi'ites pronouncing on social and religious principles, often far different from those of the Sunnites who constitute the great majority in the Moslem world. The first page of the book has a few lines in the Ayatollah's own hand, with his signature and his seal, to the effect that all these texts are the faithful reflection of his ideas and must be put into practice by every Shi'ite Moslem.

The principles presented in them give answers to all the daily problems of the faithful. The highest spiritual dignitaries (*Modjtahed*) who preach and propagate them are among the most erudite and virtuous of the learned of Islam. Contrary to the practice of the Catholic

Church, they are not chosen through a hierarchical election or by a consistory, but by the faithful themselves, who make their own choice of the spiritual guide whom they will obey and whose directives they will follow in matters of religious discipline. Thus, there are at all times not one but several religious authorities, among whom, however, one is de facto considered, almost unanimously, to be the supreme authority.

This religious leader, as the Ayatollah Khomeini indicates in his book, must fulfill the following criteria: he must be of the male sex, of age, intelligent, a believer in the Twelve Imams, of legitimate birth and heritage, alive, just, without interest in worldly goods, and the most erudite, i.e., the one best suited to understand and interpret the divine laws. The competence and superiority of this authority must be attested to by (1) the informed believer who is personally convinced of the master's virtues and selects him from among all others to be his supreme spiritual guide; or (2) two men well known to be just and erudite, providing however that their affirmations are not contradicted by two other persons having equal qualifications; or (3) a group of men who are authorities in matters religious, who have selected this spiritual master from among all others.

The teachings of the *Modjtahed* may be gathered orally in the course of a preachment, or reported by two just people, or heard from the mouth of someone known to be a speaker of the truth, or else gotten from a book which one is assured is by the master.

Sayings of the Ayatollah Khomeini

The Ayatollah Khomeini has set down his religious teachings in *The Explanation of Problems,* which may therefore properly be considered the perfect "breviary" of the Shi'ite Moslem, who must scrupulously follow its instructions, as it gives him the Ayatollah Khomeini's answers to all religious problems.

Its various chapters cover the social, financial, juridical, liturgical, and sexual aspects of the life of the Iranian faithful: prayer, fasting, ablutions, religious rites, food and drink, the slaughter of animals, sex life, marriage, divorce, adultery, commerce, money, inheritance, death, and so on.

Full translation of the very long and specialized original texts would have been too much for a Western reader to plow through; therefore, we have decided to select from them the parts which appear to us to be most representative. The sober, direct, and repetitive presentation of the texts, intended to make the principles easy to memorize, has been retained in the translation.

JEAN-MARIE XAVIERE

Part I

POLITICAL
AND
PHILOSOPHICAL SAYINGS

1

Islam
as a Revolutionary Religion

Islam is the religion of those who struggle for truth and justice, of those who clamor for liberty and independence. It is the school of those who fight against colonialism.

* * * *

Our one and only remedy is to bring down these corrupt and corrupting systems of government, and to overthrow the traitorous, repressive, and despotic gangs in charge. This is the duty of all Moslems in all Islamic countries; this is the way to victory for all Islamic revolutions.

* * * *

Moslems have no alternative, if they wish to correct the political balance of society, and force those in power to conform to the laws and principles of Islam, to an armed holy war against profane governments.

* * * *

Though you may not have the means to prevent heresy or fight corruption, nevertheless you must not remain silent. If they hit you in the head, protest! Resigning yourself to oppression is more immoral than oppression itself. Argue, denounce, oppose, shout. Spread the truth—that Islamic justice is not what they say it is.

* * * *

Holy war means the conquest of all non-Moslem territories. Such a war may well be declared after the formation of an Islamic government worthy of that name, at the direction of the Imam or under his orders. It will then be the duty of every ablebodied adult male to volunteer for this war of conquest, the final aim of which is to put Koranic law in power from one end of the earth to the other. But the whole world should understand that the universal supremacy of Islam is considerably different from the hegemony of other conquerors. It is therefore necessary for the Islamic government first to be created under the authority of the Imam in order that he may undertake this conquest, which will be distinguishable from all other wars of conquest, which are unjust and tyrannical and disregard the moral and civilizing principles of Islam.

4

* * * *

Who liberated our country and our people from the shame of Zoroastrianism, if not the victorious army of Islam?

* * * *

There are some of us who aren't concerned with developing an Islamic movement, but, instead, of making the pilgrimage to Mecca with their Moslem brothers, in peace and understanding. It certainly wasn't that way in the time of the Prophet. The Friday prayers were the means of mobilizing the people, of inspiring them to battle. The man who goes to war straight from the mosque is afraid of only one thing—God. Dying, poverty, and homelessness mean nothing to him; an army of men like that is a victorious army.

* * * *

Islamic faith and justice demand that within the Moslem world, anti-Islamic governments not be allowed to survive. The installation of a lay public power is equivalent to actively opposing the progress of Islamic order. Any nonreligious power, whatever form or shape it may take, is necessarily an atheistic power, the tool of Satan; it is part of our duty to stand in its path and to struggle against its effects. Such Satanic power can engender nothing but corruption on earth, the supreme evil

5

which must be pitilessly fought and rooted out. To achieve that end, we have no recourse other than to overthrow all governments that do not rest on pure Islamic principles, and are thus corrupt and corrupting, and to tear down the traitorous, rotten, unjust, and tyrannical administrative systems that serve them. That is not only our duty in Iran, but it is also the duty of all Moslems in the world, in all Moslem countries, to carry the Islamic political revolution to its final victory.

2

Islam and Colonialism

Europe [the West] is nothing but a collection of unjust dictatorships; all of humanity must strike these troublemakers with an iron hand if it wishes to regain its tranquillity. If Islamic civilization had governed the West, we would no longer have to put up with these barbaric goings-on unworthy even of wild animals.

* * * *

At a time in the West so primitive that there is no recorded history of it, when its inhabitants were still wild, and when America was still a land of half-wild redskins, the peoples of the Persian and Roman empires were forced to live under depotism, oligarchy, favoritism, and absolute rule, without the slightest participation or right to participate in their own government. It was then that God, through his prophet, sent us the laws whose scope has amazed mankind.

* * * *

The homeland of Islam, one and indivisible, was broken up by the doings of the imperialists and despotic and ambitious leaders. The Moslem people, one and indivisible, was broken up into several peoples. And when the Ottoman Empire struggled to achieve Islamic unity it was opposed by a united front of Russian, English, Austrian, and other imperialist powers, which split it up among themselves.

* * * *

Western missionaries, carrying out secret plans drawn up centuries ago, have created religious schools of their own within Moslem countries. We did not react against that, and this is what it led to: These missionaries infiltrated our villages and our countrysides, to turn our children into Christians or atheists!

* * * *

The Islamic movement met its first saboteur in the Jewish people, who are at the source of all the anti-Islamic libels and intrigues current today. Then came the turn of those even more damnable representatives of Satan, the imperialists. Within the last three centuries or more, they have invaded every Moslem country, with the intention of destroying Islam. They have been aware ever since the Crusades that only Islam, with its laws and its faith, can bar the way to their material interests and political power. They sent missionaries into Moslem cities, and there found accomplices within the universities and various information or publication centers, mobilized their Orientalist scholars in the service of imperialism—all of that only so as to distort Islamic truths.

❊ ❊ ❊ ❊

Their plan is to keep us in our backward state, to preserve our pathetic way of life, so they can exploit the tremendous wealth of our underground resources, of our land, and of our manpower. They want us to stay destitute, distracted by niggling day-to-day problems of survival, our poor living in misery, so that we will never become aware of the laws of Islam—which contain the solution to misery and poverty! All of this they have done so they can sit in their big palaces, living their stupid shallow lives!

❊ ❊ ❊ ❊

Many of these corruptions have their origin in the gang that is in power, and in the family of a despotic and capricious ruler. These are the rulers who create hotbeds of lust, prostitution and drugs, who devote the revenues of the mosque to building cinemas!

❉ ❉ ❉ ❉

Islam does not have kings or crowned princes. If that's a fault, well then, Islam is a faulty religion!

❉ ❉ ❉ ❉

What do you understand of the harmony between social life and religious principles? And, more important, just what is the social life we are talking about? Is it those hotbeds of immorality called theaters, cinemas, dancing, and music? Is it the promiscuous presence in the streets of lusting young men and women with arms, chests, and thighs bared? Is it the ludicrous wearing of a hat like the Europeans or the imitation of their habit of wine drinking? We are convinced that you have been made to lose your ability to distinguish between good and evil, in exchange for a few radio sets and ludicrous Western hats. Your attention has been attracted to the disrobed women to been seen on thoroughfares and in swimming pools. Let these shameful practices come to an end, so that the dawn of a new life may break!

❉ ❉ ❉ ❉

All governments of the world rely upon the power of their bayonets. We know of no monarchy or republic in the world today which is based upon equity and reason; all maintain themselves in power only through oppression.

❊ ❊ ❊ ❊

The leaders of our country have been so deeply influenced by the West that they have regulated the standard time of their country upon that of Europe (Greenwich Mean Time). What a nightmare!

❊ ❊ ❊ ❊

In the past century, during which European medicine and surgery have been introduced into Iran, our leaders have forgotten our traditional medicine and encouraged a handful of inexperienced young men to study this cursed European medicine. Today we realize that illnesses such as typhus, typhoid fever, and the like are curable only by traditional remedies.

❊ ❊ ❊ ❊

The clergy must undertake no functions other than religious ones which serve monotheism, virtue, the teaching of the divine laws, and the uplifting of public morals. The army must also be under the control of the clergy in order to be efficacious and useful.

❊ ❊ ❊ ❊

We [clergy] forcefully affirm that refusal to wear the veil is against the law of God and the Prophet, and a material and moral affront to the entire country. We affirm that the ludicrous use of the Western hat stands in the way of our independence and is contrary to the will of God. We affirm that coeducational schools are an obstacle to a wholesome life; they are a material and moral affront to the country and contrary to the divine will. We affirm that music engenders immorality, lust, and licentiousness, and stifles courage, valor, and the chivalrous spirit; it is forbidden by Koranic laws and must not be taught in the schools. Radio Teheran, by broadcasting Western, Oriental, and Iranian music, plays a nefarious role by introducing immorality and licentiousness into respectable families.

❊ ❊ ❊ ❊

Ulamas [religious scholars] and other ecclesiastics are not permitted to run the theology schools set up by the state. State intervention in this domain is always a pretext for the destruction of the foundations of Islam on orders of the imperialists. This happens in all Moslem countries without exception.

❊ ❊ ❊ ❊

Members of the clergy who, wearing clerical garb, cooperate in one way or another with such schools of theology must be shunned by all true Moslems. It is forbidden to associate with them, to indulge in collective prayer in their presence, to make use of their services for the repudiation of one's wife, to pay legal alms to them, to invite them to officiate at funeral ceremonies, or to listen to their sermons at meetings organized by the state with the sole intent of having them preach lies and diabolical anti-Islamic thoughts.

* * * *

When the imperialists, the traitorous and tyrannical governors, the Jews, the Christians, and the materialists have all gotten together to distort the truths of Islam and mislead the Moslem peoples, it is more than ever our duty and responsibility to carry out an active propaganda campaign.

* * * *

We see today that the Jews—may God bring them down!—have manipulated the editions of the Koran published in their occupied zones. We have to protest, to make everyone understand that these Jews are bent upon the destruction of Islam and the establishment of a universal Jewish government. And since they are a cunning and active people, I fear—may God forever protect us from it!—that sooner or later they may succeed in attaining this goal, that through the weakness of some among us we may one day find ourselves under Jewish rule—God preserve us from it!

* * * *

Some scholarly Orientalists, agents in the pay of the imperialists, are working to transform the Islamic truths. The missionaries, those other agents of imperalism, are also busy throughout the Moslem world in perverting our youth, not by converting them to their own religion, but by corrupting them. And that is the very thing the imperialists are after. In Teheran itself, propaganda centers for Christianity, Zionism, and Bahaism, have been set up for the sole purpose of luring the faithful away from the commandments of Islam. Is it not our duty to destroy all these hotbeds of danger to Islam?

3

The Islamic Republic

An Islamic government cannot be totalitarian or despotic, but is constitutional and democratic. In this democracy, however, the laws are not made by the will of the people, but only by the Koran and the Sunna [Traditions] of the Prophet. The constitution, the civil code, and the criminal code should be inspired only by Islamic laws contained in the Koran and transcribed by the Prophet. Islamic government is the government of divine right, and its laws cannot be changed, modified, or contested.

❋ ❋ ❋ ❋

In any self-respecting Islamic government, the legislative, executive, and judicial branches are replaced by a Religious Planning Council. The council keeps each cabinet department informed of the Islamic laws affecting it, indicates what its program must be in conformity with religious law, and on the basis of the

totality of these programs establishes general
policy for the whole country.

* * * *

The Islamic government is subject to the
law of Islam, which comes neither from the
people nor from its representatives, but directly from God and His divine will. Koranic law,
which is nothing other than divine law, consti-
tutes the essence of any Islamic government
and unfailingly governs all individuals who are
a part of it. The Prophet, the Caliphs [spiritu-
al heads of Islam], and the people all owe absolute obedience to these eternal laws of the
Almighty, transmitted to mortals through the
Koran and the Prophet, which remain immuta-
ble until the end of time.

* * * *

It is often proclaimed that religion must
be separated from politics, and that the ecclesi-
astical world should keep out of affairs of state.
It is proclaimed that high Moslem clerical authorities have no business mixing into the social and political decisions of the government.
Such proclamations can come only from atheists; they are dictated and spread by imperialists. Was politics separate from religion in the
time of the Prophet (God salute him, him and
his faithful!)? Was there a distinction at that
time between the religious and the high func-
tionaries of the state? Were religious and tem-
poral powers separate in the times of the

Caliphs? Those are aberrations invented by the imperialists with a view to turning the clergy away from the material and social life of Moslem peoples, and thus to getting a free hand to pillage their wealth.

* * * *

Think of it—a political clergy! Well, why not? The Prophet was a politician!

* * * *

He (the Prophet) appointed governors to provinces, formed tribunals and named judges, set up embassies in other countries, and sent ambassadors to other tribes and kings ... in short, all the normal functions of government.

* * * *

In order to ensure the unity of the Moslem people, to liberate the Islamic homeland from the domination or the influence of imperialists, we have no other way out than to form a true Islamic government, do whatever is necessary to overthrow the other tyrannical pseudo-Moslem governments put in place by foreigners, and once this goal is attained to install *the* universal Islamic government.

* * * *

We have nothing against going to the moon, or setting up atomic installations. But we too have a mission to accomplish: the mission of serving Islam and making its sacred principles known to the entire world, in the hope that all the monarchs and presidents of republics throughout the Moslem world will finally recognize that our cause is just, and by that very fact become submissive to us. Naturally, we have no desire to strip them of their functions; we will allow them to retain power, provided they show themselves to be obedient and worthy of our confidence.

❉ ❉ ❉ ❉

If the enemy attacks the borders of an Islamic country, it is the sacred duty of all Moslems in the world to defend it by every means in their power, by giving of their wealth or of their persons. They need await no permission to fulfill this duty.

❉ ❉ ❉ ❉

If, within a Moslem country, diabolical foreign plans are fomented, and if there is any fear that these may lead to foreign domination, it is the duty of every Moslem to work against such plans.

❉ ❉ ❉ ❉

If, as a result of the political, economic, or commercial influence of foreigners, there is the risk of seeing the latter gain control over the destinies of Islamic countries, it is the duty of every Moslem to defend the interests at stake and bar the path to any foreign intrusion.

* * * *

If there is a justified fear that the diplomatic relations of Moslem states with foreign states might lead to the predominance of the latter within Moslem countries, even if such predominance be only political or economic, all Moslems must oppose such a situation with force, and compel the Islamic governments to sever such diplomatic relations.

* * * *

If there comes to be a justified concern that commercial relations with foreigners might be harmful to Islamic markets and lead to commercial or economic dependence, such relations must be broken off and such commerce proclaimed to be religiously illicit.

* * * *

If establishing political or commercial relations between a Moslem and a non-Moslem country is not in the interests of Islam and Moslems, such relations are forbidden; if a country allows them, it is the duty of all other Moslem countries to force it by every means within their power to sever such relations.

* * * *

If certain chiefs of state of Moslem countries or certain members of parliament favor a foreign political, economic, or military influence, which is inevitably against the interests of Islam and of all Moslems, they must for such treason be removed from their functions, whatever these may be, even though they may have acceded to them through entirely legal means. It is the duty of all Moslems to punish such individuals by ever possible means.

* * * *

It is forbidden for any Moslem state to have commercial and diplomatic relations with countries which play the role of puppets for the great powers—as is the case with Israel—and it is the duty of all Moslems to oppose such relations by every means available; any businessman having commercial dealings with Israel, its representatives, or its agents is a traitor to Islam and to all other Moslems, because he is contributing to the destruction of Islam. It is the duty of all Moslems to sever their relations with such traitors, whether they be states or businessmen, with a view to forcing them to repent.

* * * *

All the laws approved and passed until now by the two chambers of the Iranian Parliament, on the orders of foreign agents—God punish them!—contrary to the texts of the Koran and the law of the Holy Prophet of Islam are hereby proclaimed null and void from the Islamic viewpoint. It is the duty of all the faithful to turn against all those who supported them, to isolate such people, not to rub elbows with them or have any business dealings with them, and to consider them as malefactors. Even going near them is in itself a cardinal sin.

4

The Rule of the Clergy

If religious experts of wisdom and justice devoted themselves to the Islamic law and to setting up an Islamic state, never again would the people go hungry.

* * * *

It is written that "the clergy rule the sultans." If the sultans are obedient to Islam, then they should also be obedient to the clergy; they should ask the clergy for laws and regulations and advice on how to apply them. In this way the clergy are the real leaders and power belongs to them, officially.

* * * *

You (the clergy) have the duty to establish an Islamic state. Have confidence in yourselves: you are perfectly capable of assuming that burden. We will do as the colonialists did three or four hundred years ago—they started from nothing and got to this point. We too will start from nothing. Don't let yourselves be intimidated by a handful of your fellow countrymen who have sold out to the West, who are the valets of imperialism. Explain to the people that the clergy are not going to sit in a corner at Qom or An Najaf studying unimportant matters like the rules governing the menstruation of women, and cutting themselves off from politics because "religion and politics should be separate."

* * * *

Are those who govern in Moslem countries these days any more capable than we are? Who among them has more aptitude than the average man? Many of them never even went to school ... Mr. Reza* was nothing but an uneducated buck private. Historically this has often been the case. Many despots and absolute rulers had neither the aptitude to run a country, nor common sense, nor knowledge nor wisdom. Harun al-Rashid† or others like him, what did they go through in the way of an education? To administer laws and govern a country, you need a solid educational grounding.

* * * *

---

*Reza Shah, the Shah's father.
†A great Caliph of Baghdad in the ninth century.

In certain cases deception is necessary for the maintenance of Islam and of religion in general; without it faith could not survive.

* * * *

If anyone, in the guise of pursuing Islamic justice, interprets the Law in a manner contrary to the divine will, he has committed the sin of innovation. Learned men are bound to condemn him or they will themselves be condemned.

* * * *

Given that the clergy occupy a lower position (than the Prophet or the Imam), should they therefore punish an offense less severely? Can we say that the Prophet ought to order a hundred and fifty lashes, Ali a hundred lashes, and the clergy only fifty, in a case when the penalty should be one hundred lashes? No. The chief magistrate possesses executive power that is always in accordance with divine standards, whether he be the Prophet, Ali, or their duly constituted representative.

5

The Imam

We need a head of government who is not at the mercy of his lust and other temptations. We need someone to govern us for whom all are equal, for whom all enjoy the same rights and obligations; someone who doesn't indulge in favoritism, who regards his family in the same light as others, who will cut off his son's hands if he steals, and execute his brothers and sisters if they sell heroin.

* * * *

As far as function and rank are concerned, there is no difference between the guardian of a minor and the guardian of an entire people. Leading the government or indeed occupying any official position is like the Imam and his appointees taking care of children.

* * * *

The great scholars, those "fortresses of Islam," are the embodiment of Islamic faith as well as its guardians. They affirm Islamic principles in their emotional and moving sermons and through the special nature of their leadership. That's why, when after a long life, perhaps even more than a hundred years, they die, that death is a great blow to Islam, and why the faithful experience an immense lack in their absence. But if it's a question of my death, I who do nothing but sit in a corner of my house studying, what lack will the faithful feel in my absence?

* * * *

The Imams were shining lights in the darkness of the heavens, infinitely gifted and by birth and nature superior to other men— much so that even the angel Gabriel declared, "If I came too close to them, I would be burned."

* * * *

The leaders of the USSR and of England and the president of the United States are invested with power (like the Imam), but they are infidels. They wield their political power and influence in order to fulfill sordid personal ambitions, which they accomplish by administering inhuman laws and using inhuman politi-

26

cal methods. But the Imam and the clergy have the duty to use the political apparatus to apply the laws of God and to bring about a system of equality for the benefit of the people. Governing means nothing for them except pain and difficulty, but what can they do? The rule of the clergy is an obligation they must fulfill.

❋ ❋ ❋ ❋

Since the Almighty did not designate anyone by name to form the Islamic government in the absence of the hidden Imam [the Twelfth Imam], what are we to do? But while God did not name anyone, He intended that the virtues characteristic of Islamic governments from the dawn of Islam to the reign of the Twelfth Imam be perpetuated. These virtues, these qualities, represented by perfect knowledge of law and justice, are to be found in many of the religious learned of our time. If those learned come together, they will be able to establish the authority that will bring about universal justice. If a competent man, combining in himself these supreme virtues, appears and founds a true Islamic government, it means that he has been invested by the Almighty with the same mandate as the Holy Prophet to lead the people; therefore, it is the people's absolute duty to follow him.

6

Islamic Justice

In an Islamic government, all people are under the protection of the law. No one may endanger their safety, break into their houses, arrest them, imprison or exile them, or summarily execute them on the basis of a simple accusation or suspicion. Under such a government, everyone can have full confidence in the law of the Prophet, and no judge or dignitary dare act contrary to it.

❖　❖　❖　❖

The person who governs the Moslem community must always have its interests at heart and not his own. This is why Islam has put so many people to death: to safeguard the interests of the Moslem community. Islam has obliterated many tribes because they were sources of corruption and harmful to the welfare of Moslems.

❈ ❈ ❈ ❈

Moslems are forbidden to seek redress of their grievances from the executive or judiciary of improperly consituted governments. They are forbidden to have legal recourse to kings or other despotic administrations, or to the judges that are appointed by them, even if they have legal rights to defend. A person whose son has been killed or whose house has been burgled may not seek justice from such courts, even if he is in the right and has conclusive evidence.

❈ ❈ ❈ ❈

Islam has precepts for everything that concerns man and society. These come from the Almighty and are transmitted to men by His Prophet and Messenger. One may well be surprised by the majesty of these commandments, which cover every aspect of life, from conception to interment! There is no subject upon which Islam has not expressed its judgment.

❈ ❈ ❈ ❈

The Islamic republic is a government according to the Law and the wise men and theological experts of the clergy are therefore responsible for it. It is they who must watch over all aspects of administration and planning. In administering the laws of God in such matters as taxes and property for example, they must be trusted. Accordingly they must not allow delay in the execution of the Islamic laws, nor must they be over lenient or over severe. If a member of the clergy wishes to inflict a penalty on someone, he must do so publicly, according to established practice, and lash him the specified number of times, without insulting him or slapping him or imprisoning him even for a single day.

* * * *

Islamic justice is based on simplicity and ease. It settles all criminal or civil complaints in the most convenient, elementary, and expeditious way possible. All that is required is for an Islamic judge, with a pen and inkwell and two or three enforcers, to go into a town, come to his verdict on any kind of case, and have it immediately carried out. Look at the present cost in time and money in Western society with all its judicial procedures surrounding any judgment, in the name of principles alien to Islam!

* * * *

If the punitive laws of Islam were applied for only one year, all the devastating injustices and immoralities would be uprooted. Misdeeds must be punished by the law of retaliation: cut off the hands of the thief; kill the murderer instead of putting him in prison; flog the adulterous woman or man. Your concerns, your "humanitarian" scruples are more childish than reasonable. Under the terms of Koranic law, any judge fulfilling the seven requirements (that he have reached puberty, be a believer, know the Koranic laws perfectly, be just, and not be affected by amnesia, or be a bastard, or be of the female sex) is qualified to dispense justice in any type of case. He can thus judge and dispose of twenty trials in a single day, whereas Occidental justice might take years to argue them out.

✳ ✳ ✳ ✳

Ali [son-in-law of Mohammed], having cut off the hands of two thieves, treated their wounds and offered them his hospitality, and this affected them so much that became utterly devoted to him; or again when he heard that the marauding army of Muawiyah had abused a woman of one of the tribes, he was so upset and moved to pity that he declared: "If a man died after such an occurrence, no one could blame him." And yet, despite a nature as sensitive as that, Ali bared his sword and hacked the perpetrators to pieces. This is the meaning of justice.

7

Youth

—◦————————————————————◦—

Students have got their eyes open. If you present them with [the case for an Islamic republic], they wil embrace it eagerly. Our students are against despotism, against repressive and colonialist authorities, against the ruffians who pillage the property of the people, against the liars who consume impurities. There is no student or university that opposes an Islam founded on teachings such as ours and run according to social principles such as ours.

✣   ✣   ✣   ✣

Our young people have the duty to rip the turban from the heads of those who, by pretending to be holy men and religious experts of Islam, are causing so much corruption among Moslems. I don't know if our youth is still alive! In my day it was never thus. Why don't they rip off those turbans? I don't say we should kill them, they are not worth killing.

But our brave youth must see to it that such mullahs do not appear in public wearing the turban. It's not necessary to hit them too much, but those turbans must come off!

* * * *

Put aside your sadness and resignation! Improve your programs and methods of spreading Islam! Make greater efforts to give it a fair presentation! Do your part: be the front-runners in setting up an Islamic republic. Put your hands in the hands of fighting and independent peoples!

* * * *

Young boys or girls in full sexual effervescence are kept from getting married before they reach the legal age of majority. This is against the intention of divine laws. Why should the marriage of pubescent girls and boys be forbidden because they are still minors, when they are allowed to listen to the radio and to sexually arousing music?

* * * *

You, young people of the new generation, try to think more clearly. Stop turning toward science and its laws which have led so many among you to neglect your major responsibilities! Come to the help of Islam! Save the Moslems! The missionaries of different denominations, who are in the service of the imperialists just as their local agents are, have spread to the four corners of the country to turn our youth away from the path of righteousness and keep them from the service of Islam. Save that youth!

8

Media and Propaganda

We have a duty to create an Islamic republic and to that end our first obligation is the creation of a system of propaganda. This has always been the way things work. Once a few people sit down together, think matters out together, make decisions, it follows that propaganda will emerge. Then little by little others who think the same way are attracted to the group and it increases in size. Ultimately the group and its propaganda becomes a force that can infiltrate a huge system of government or even bring about its downfall.

* * * *

Radio and television are allowed if they are used for the broadcasting of news or sermons, for the spreading of good educational material, for publicizing the products and curiosities of the planet; but they must prohibit singing, music, anti-Islamic laws, the lauding of tyrants, mendacious words, and broadcasts which spread doubt and undermine virtue.

* * * *

Since the use of radio and television sets is not carried out in conformity with the above-mentioned principles, the trade in them is limited to those who will put them to good use and who will see to it that others follow in the same path.

Part II

SOCIAL
AND
RELIGIOUS SAYINGS

9

On the Manner of Urinating and Defecating

It is required that everyone, when urinating or defecating, hide his sexual parts from all pubescent persons, even his sister or his mother, as well as from any feebleminded person or children too young to understand. But husband and wife are not required to hide them from each other.

❋ ❋ ❋ ❋

It is not indispensable to hide one's genitals with anything in particular; one's hand is enough.

❋ ❋ ❋ ❋

When defecating or urinating, one must squat in such a way as neither to face Mecca nor to turn one's back upon it.

* * * *

It is not sufficient to turn one's sex organ away, while oneself facing or turning one's back on Mecca; and one's privates must never be exposed either facing Mecca or facing directly away from Mecca.

* * * *

Urinating and defecating are forbidden in four places: blind alleys, except with the permission of those living along them; the property of a person who has not given permission to do so; places of worship, such as certain *medersas;* graves of believers, unless one does so as an insult to them.

* * * *

In three cases, it is absolutely necessary to purify one's anus with water: when the excrement has been expelled with other impurities, such as blood, for example; when some impure thing has grazed the anus; when the anal opening has been soiled more than usual.

Apart from these three cases, one may either wash one's anus with water or wipe it with some fabric or a stone.

* * * *

The urinary orifice can be cleaned off only with water, and it is enough to wash it just one time after urinating. But those in whom the urine comes out through some other orifice would do better to wash that orifice at least twice. This must be observed by women as well.

*   *   *   *

It is not necessary to wipe one's anus with three stones or three pieces of fabric: a single stone or single piece of fabric is enough. But if one wipes it with a bone, or any sacred object, such as, for example, a paper having the name of God on it, one may not say his prayers while in this state.

*   *   *   *

It is preferable, for urinating or defecating, to squat down in an isolated place; it is also preferable to go into this place with the left foot first, and come out of it with the right foot first; it is recommended that one keep his head covered while evacuating, and have the weight of his body carried by the left foot.

*   *   *   *

During evacuation, one must not squat facing the sun or the moon, unless one's genitals are covered. While defecating, one must also avoid squatting exposed to the wind, or in public places, or at the door of one's house, or under a fruit tree. At the time of evacuation, one must also avoid eating, dallying, or washing one's anus with the right hand. Finally, one must avoid talking, unless one is absolutely forced to or is addressing a prayer to God.

* * * *

It is better to avoid urinating standing up, or urinating onto hard ground, or into an animal hole, or into water, especially stagnant water.

* * * *

It is recommended not to hold back the need to urinate or defecate, especially if it hurts.

* * * *

It is recommended to urinate before praying, before going to bed, before having sexual intercourse, and after ejaculating.

* * * *

After urination, one must first wash the anus if it has been soiled by urine; then one must press three times with the middle finger of his left hand on the part between the anus and the base of the penis; then one must put his thumb on top of the penis and his index finger on the bottom and pull the skin forward three times as far as the circumcision ring; and after that three times squeeze the tip of the penis.

❊ ❊ ❊ ❊

A woman has no special instructions to follow after urinating; if she afterward notes some moisture at the vaginal orifice which she cannot judge as pure or impure, the said moisture remains pure and in no wise stands in the way of her performing ablutions or praying.

10

On the Manner of
Eating and Drinking

There are eighteen principles to be observed at mealtimes: washing one's hands before the meal; washing and drying one's hands after the meal; the head of the house beginning eating before any of his guests and finishing after them; he must wash his hands before the meal ahead of the others, and be followed by the person who sits at his right, and then the next, and so on, until reaching the one seated at his left; beginning the meal by invoking the name of God; but if several courses are served, it is recommended that this be repeated before each course; taking with one's right hand; eating with three fingers, leaving the other two free; taking small quantities of food in each mouthful; stretching the meal out as long as possible; chewing one's food at length; praising God at the end of the meal; licking one's fingers; cleaning one's teeth after the meal with a toothpick, which must not be made of pomegranate wood, basil wood, reed, or palm leaves; gathering up the remains of the meal in order to eat them later, but if the meal is eaten in the desert it is better to leave such remains for the birds and animals; eating at the beginning of the day and at nightfall, and abstaining therefrom during the day and during the night; resting on one's back after eating, and putting the right leg over the left leg; taking salt at the beginning and the end of the meal; washing all fruit before eating it.

* * * *

There are eleven things to be avoided during meals: eating when one is not hungry; eating too much, which is frowned upon by the Almighty; watching others while eating; eating things that are too hot; blowing on a dish or into a glass to cool the food or drink; starting to eat as soon as the bread has been put on the table; cutting bread with a knife; putting bread under one's plate; cleaning a meat bone so that there is nothing left on it; peeling fruit; throwing away half-eaten fruit.

* * * *

There are six principles to be observed while drinking water: sucking it up rather than gulping it down; drinking upright invoking the name of God before and after drinking; drinking in three steps; drinking of one's own free will; recalling the martyrdom of Hazrat Aba Abdollah and his family, and cursing their murderers, after drinking.

* * * *

There are five things to be avoided during the absorption of water: drinking to excess; drinking after a heavy meal; drinking standing up during the night; taking the water jug in one's left hand; drinking from a place where the jug is chipped or broken or at the location of the handle

* * * *

Among the organs of fowl, game, domestic animals, fish, and so on whose flesh of you are permitted to eat, there are fifteen which are proscribed: blood; excrement; the penis; the vagina; the uterus; the glands; the testicles; the central part of the brain; the little chick-pea-shaped ball at the back side of the brain; the nerves located on either side of the spinal column; the gallbladder; the liver; the bladder; the eye; matter accumulated under the claws.

* * * *

It is forbidden to consume the excrement of animals or their nasal secretions. But if such are mixed in minute proportions into other foods their consumption is not forbidden.

✻ ✻ ✻ ✻

The meat of horses, mules, or donkeys is not recommended. It is strictly forbidden if the animal was sodomized while alive by a man. In that case, the animal must be taken outside the city and sold.

✻ ✻ ✻ ✻

If one commits an act of sodomy with a cow, a ewe, or a camel, their urine and their excrements become impure, and even their milk may no longer be consumed. The animal must then be killed as quickly as possible and burned, and the price of it paid to its owner by him who sodomized it.

✻ ✻ ✻ ✻

Drinking wine or alcoholic beverages is a mortal sin, and is strictly forbidden. Whoever consumes an alcoholic beverage retains only a part of his soul, that part of it which is deformed and nasty; he is damned by God, His archangels, His prophets, and His believers. Such a man's daily prayers are rejected by God for forty days. On the day of the resurrection of the dead, his face will turn black, his tongue will hang out of his mouth, his saliva will run down his chest, and he will remain forever thirsty.

11

On Purity and Impurity*

There are eleven things which are impure: urine, excrement, sperm, bones, blood, dogs, pigs, non-Moslem men and women, wine, beer, and the sweat of the excrement-eating camel.

❋　❋　❋　❋

The urine and feces of man and any animal whose blood spurts when a vein or artery of its body is opened† are impure. But flyspecks or the droppings of mosquitoes or other such

---

*What is referred to here is not impurity in general, but rather that group of elements described in paragraph 1 of this chapter, things which may not be eaten, and which, if they come into contact with the body of one of the faithful, keep the latter from being able to perform his religious duties (prayer, fasting, pilgrimage, reading of Holy Writ, participation in funeral ceremonies, and so on) so long as he has not undergone purification through the performance of small or great ablutions.

†This means animals such as cattle and sheep, as opposed to fish, frogs, insects, and the like.

small insects whose blood does not gush are pure.

❊   ❊   ❊   ❊

The urine and feces of any excrement-eating animal are impure. This is equally true of the urine and feces of any animal which has been sexually possessed by a human; and of the urine and feces of sheep which have been fed on sow's milk.

❊   ❊   ❊   ❊

The sperm of any animal whose blood spurts when its throat is cut is impure.

❊   ❊   ❊   ❊

The bones of an animal found dead or an animal slaughtered otherwise than according to Moslem rites are impure; fish, on the other hand, is never impure, even if found dead in the water, for its blood does not spurt.

❊   ❊   ❊   ❊

The hairs, bones, and teeth of dead animals are pure, unless they come from animals such as the dog which are impure in themselves.

❊   ❊   ❊   ❊

The egg taken from the entrails of a chicken is not impure, provided its shell is efficiently hard. However, it must be washed before being eaten.

* * * *

The meat, fat, and skins on sale in a Moslem bazaar or being handled by a Moslem are pure, unless such products come from animals which were not slaughtered according to the Moslem rites

* * * *

The blood of man and of any animal whose blood spurts when the throat is cut is impure; on the other hand, the blood of the fish, mosquito, or any other animal whose blood does not spurt remains pure.

* * * *

The blood that may flow out between one's teeth is pure if diluted with saliva; it is permitted to swallow that saliva.

Blood coagulated and accumulated under the nails or in any other part of the human body is pure if its appearance has been so modified that one can no longer call it blood; if that is not the case, every effort must be made to rid oneself of it before performing one's ablutions.

❋ ❋ ❋ ❋

The pus of a healing wound is pure, provided one can be sure it is not mixed with blood.

❋ ❋ ❋ ❋

Dog and pig, unless they live in water, are impure, as are their hairs, their bones, their claws, and their excrements; on the other hand, sea dogs and pigs are pure.

❋ ❋ ❋ ❋

Every part of the body of a non-Moslem individual is impure, even the hair on his hand and his body hair, his nails, and all the secretions of his body.

❋ ❋ ❋ ❋

Any man or woman who denies the existence of God, or believes in His partners [the Christian Trinity], or else does not believe in His Prophet Mohammed, is impure (in the same way as are excrement, urine, dog, and wine). He is so even if he doubts any one of these principles.

❋ ❋ ❋ ❋

A child who has not reached puberty is impure if his parents and grandparents are not

Moslems, but if he has one Moslem in his ancestry he is pure.

* * * *

A Moslem who insults one of the Twelve Imans or declares himself their enemy is impure.

* * * *

Wine and all other intoxicating beverages are impure, but opium and hashish are not.

* * * *

Beer is impure, but brewer's yeast is not.

* * * *

The sweat of an excrement-eating animal is impure; the sweat of other animals, which do not eat the same detritus, is not.

* * * *

The sweat of a man who has just ejaculated is not impure; yet it is preferable for him not to pray so long as his body or his clothing retain traces of that sweat.

* * * *

If a man has had sexual relations with his wife during periods of prescribed abstinence, such as the fast of Ramadan, he must avoid saying his prayers so long as he still has upon him the traces of postcoital sweat.

✻ ✻ ✻ ✻

If a part of the body that is sweating comes into contact with something impure and the sweat runs onto other parts of the body, all such parts become impure, although the rest of the body remains pure.

✻ ✻ ✻ ✻

Bloodstained nasal secretions or expectorations are impure, whereas those which have not been soiled by blood are pure; if the nasal secretions or the expectoration touch the nose or mouth even lightly the part of the skin which has been so touched must be purified; but the untouched part remains pure.

✻ ✻ ✻ ✻

An object which enters a human body and comes into contact with something impure (stool or blood) remains pure when withdrawn from that body if it has no traces of the impure matter left upon it; thus, the instrument introduced into the rectum for an enema or the surgeon's scalpel are not impure if they bear no trace of these impurities. The same applies to saliva or nasal secretions which mix with blood inside the mouth or nose, but show no trace of it when they are expectorated.

❀ ❀ ❀ ❀

It is forbidden to touch a page of the Koran with anything impure; if such a thing should happen, the page must immediately be washed.

❀ ❀ ❀ ❀

It is forbidden to place upon the Koran such impure matter as blood or human or animal bones if the matter is dried; should the matter already have been placed on it, it must absolutely be removed.

❀ ❀ ❀ ❀

It is forbidden to write out verses of the Koran with impure ink, even though one write but one letter thereof. In case it has already been done, it must be washed away or erased with a knife or some other sharp instrument.

❀ ❀ ❀ ❀

One must avoid giving the Koran to an infidel; it is even recommended that it be forcibly taken away from him if he already has it in his hands.

❀ ❀ ❀ ❀

If a page of the Koran, or a piece of paper with the name of God or the Prophet or one of the Imams on it should fall into a toilet, it is absolutely indispensable to withdraw it from there, even if this should prove costly. In case this is impossible, such a toilet must never again be used until it has been ascertained that the paper has rotted away.

* * * *

It is forbidden to eat or drink anything that is impure; it is also forbidden to give anything impure to children to eat, whether or not it may be harmful to them; but it is not forbidden to feed children food which has been only indirectly touched by something impure.

* * * *

It is not required that one point out to a person that he is eating impure food or that he is praying while wearing impure clothing.

* * * *

If the head of a household notices during the course of a meal that one or more of the dishes being served are impure, he must impart this information to his guests; but if it is one of the guests who notices it, he is not obliged to do the same.

12

On Purification

* * *

There are eleven elements or procedures which are purifying, that is, which erase impurities and make bodies and objects pure again: water; earth; sun; transmutation; reduction of grape juice by two-thirds; transfer; Islam; dependence; elimination of the impure object; keeping an animal which normally eats excrement from doing so for a specific period of time; absence of the Moslem.

Here are explanations for each element:

Water is purifying if it fulfills the following four conditions: it is pure (thus are watermelon juice and rose water not purifying); it is clean; after having been used to wash something impure, it has not taken on the odor, color, or taste of that impure thing; after such washing, the remains of excrement or other detritus have left no traces in it.

An impure dish or container must be washed three times to regain its purity; but a container which has been licked by a dog or been used to give a dog his food or drink in, before being twice washed in water, must be rubbed first with earth. If a pig has used it, the dish must be washed seven times in succession but it need not be rubbed with earth. A container or glass which has held wine, and therefore is impure, must be washed three times, but it is better to wash it seven times. An oven which has become impure for having been urinated in regains its purity after twice being filled with water enough to cover all its sides. But if it has become impure from the contact of some other matter, such as excrement, it is enough to fill it with water once, after having removed the impure matter. If a thing becomes impure through having been soiled by the urine of a milk-fed boy (less than two years old), who has not drunk sow's milk, it is enough to wash it all over one time to purify it. Yet it is wise to wash it again a second time.

If the surface of a grain of wheat or rice or a piece of soap is soiled by some impurity, it is enough to plunge it into the amount of water required for purification in order for it to be pure again, but if the impurity has penetrated beneath its surface, this measure is not enough. If one cannot be absolutely sure that the impurity has penetrated deeply into the soap, the latter remains pure. Any impure object becomes pure only when the impure matter has been completely eliminated from it, but if the odor or color of the impure matter remains that makes no difference. The bits of impure food that remains between one's teeth after eating the food become pure if one washes his mouth with water so that all the impure remains are washed away.

If lump sugar has been made from impure melted sugar, the lump sugar remains impure even if placed in stagnant or running water.

Earth purifies the sole of the foot or shoe soiled with impurity, if it fulfills the following three conditions: it is pure; it is dry; and there is enough of it to eliminate the impure element (blood, urine, excrement, and such) from the sole of the foot or shoe. The earth may be muddy, firm, sandy, or pebbly; it is not enough to walk on a rug, or carpet, or grass, to purify the foot or shoe, as it is also not enough to walk on asphalt or flooring.

To purify the sole of the foot or shoe soiled by an impurity, one must take at least fifteen steps, even if the impurity disappears before fifteen steps.

For those who walk on their hands or knees, taking fifteen steps is not enough to purify their palms or their knees soiled by an impurity. The same applies to canes, crutches, horseshoes, wagon wheels, and so on. If, after taking the fifteen steps, small bits of excrement or other detritus remain, they must be carefully removed, but the persistence of their odor or color makes no difference. The inside of the shoe, or the part of the sole of the foot which does not touch the ground, will not be purified by walking, and this also applies to socks, unless the part of the sock covering the sole of the foot is made of leather or hide.

Sun has purifying action on impure elements such as the ground, a building, doors, windows, nails stuck into walls, if the following six conditions are all fulfilled: that the impure object be moist (if it is dry, it must be moistened so the sun may dry it); that the impurity is removed before the object is exposed to the rays of the sun; that these rays are not filtered through a curtain or through clouds, for example, unless it be an extremely thin cloud; that the impure object is dried exclusively by the rays of the sun, and not by the combined effect of sun and wind; that the sun dries all of the impure part of a building at one time (the facade may not be purified first, and the other walls only later); and, finally, that there is no intermediate element, such as air, within the thickness of the wall. If the sun has dried out impure ground, but later there is reason to question whether at the time it was moist or dry, or whether its moisture disappeared exclusively through the action of the rays of the sun or because of other factors, that ground remains impure; the same applies to ground or a building about which one cannot be sure that the impurities were removed from it before it was exposed to the sun, or whether the rays of the sun were able to play upon it directly. If only one of the walls was exposed to the sun, the other remains impure, unless the wall is so thin that drying one also dries the other.

Transmutation is a reaction by virtue of which an impure element is so completely transformed that it becomes something pure. This is the case of impure wood which in burning becomes transformed into pure ash, or of a dog which after being buried in saline ground turns into salt; but it does not apply to impure wheat which is made into flour or bread. Wine which turns to vinegar, whether on its own or due to the addition of salt or vinegar, is pure, but vinegar resulting from wine made of grapes soiled by urine or excrement, or from wine which has been mixed with such impurities, remains impure. Vinegar made with impure grapes, raisins, or dates remains impure. There is no objection to straw or small bits of vine or date tree remaining among the grapes or the raisins being transformed into vinegar; nor is there any objection to cucumbers or eggplants being added to the dates, raisins, or grapes before they are made into vinegar.

Reduction of grape juice by two-thirds is purifying. Boiled grape juice is not impure even before having been reduced by two-thirds, but its consumption is forbidden if it is proven that it is intoxicating, in which case the juice can be purified only when it is turned into vinegar. The juice of an unripe bunch of grapes, even if the bunch has one or two ripe grapes on it, may be consumed, on condition that it first be boiled and that the sweet taste of the grape has disappeared.

Transfer is the operation by which the blood of a human being or any other animal the blood of which spurts when its throat is cut becomes pure by being transferred into the body of an insect the blood of which does not gush and becoming absorbed into the blood of the latter. On the other hand, human blood sucked by a leech remains impure even after its transfer into the body of the leech because it does not become absorbed into the blood of the leech.

If a person crushes a mosquito on his skin and cannot determine whether the blood therefrom is the insect's or his own, this blood is pure; but if the time between the bite and the death of the mosquito is so short that no such distinction can be made, the blood is impure.

Islam. A non-Moslem man or woman who becomes a convert to Islam automatically has a pure body, and pure saliva, nasal secretions, and perspiration. As for converts' clothing, if it has been in contact with their sweating bodies before they became converted, it remains impure.

Dependence means the purification of one impure object being subject to the purification of another impure object. In the case of wine being turned into vinegar, the container having held the wine becomes pure once more up to the level reached by the wine turned vinegar. Thus, the piece of wood or stone on which mortuary ablutions are made, the fabric covering the genitals of the deceased, the hand of the person who has performed these ablutions, and the soap with which the corpse was washed, all become pure upon completion of the ritual.

The body of an animal or insect which was directly in contact with some impurity such as blood, or indirectly with impure water, becomes pure again as soon as the impure element is eliminated. The same holds true for the inside of the human mouth or nose. This means that if some blood runs out between one's teeth and dissolves in saliva, it is not necessary to wash one's mouth; if artificial teeth have been soiled by some impure matter, they must be taken out and washed. If bits of food remain between one's teeth and the inside of one's mouth bleeds, these bits of food are pure so long as one cannot be certain that the blood has touched them.

Keeping an animal which normally eats excrement from doing so for a specific period of time. The urine and feces of such an animal are impure; in order for them to become pure, such animals must be kept from eating human excrement for forty days for a camel, twenty days for cattle, ten days for sheep, seven or five days for a turkey, and three days for a chicken.

Absence of the Moslem. If the clothing, kitchen utensils, or rugs belonging to a Moslem have been soiled by impure matter, and their owner is absent, they may not automatically be considered to be impure so long as one is not sure that they were not washed and purified before he left, or that they did not happen to fall into running water which purified them.

❖ ❖ ❖ ❖

If one is certain that an object soiled by some impure matter has been purified, or if two trustworthy witnesses confirm that it has, the object becomes pure once again. This is also true of an impure object about which its owner asserts that it has been purified or that a Moslem has washed it, even if it cannot be established that he did so according to ritual.

* * * *

One must not eat or drink out of any container made of pigskin or dog's hide, or any container made from the bone of any animal.

* * * *

The remains of the food of dogs, pigs, and non-Moslem men and women are impure; the remains of the food of animals the flesh of which may be eaten are not impure, but it is nevertheless better to abstain therefrom.

13

On the Nature of Water

There are two kinds of water: pure water, and water that is "in solution," such as, for instance, watermelon juice or attar of roses, or muddy water. Pure water is divided into five categories: stagnant water large enough in quantity to be purified; stagnant water in insufficient quantity; running water; rainwater; and well water.

❊ ❊ ❊ ❊

Kor, or purifying water, is the quantity of water held in a container the length, width, and depth of which each are 3½ vadjabs.* This quantity of water should weigh 128 maunds less 20 miskals.†

❊ ❊ ❊ ❊

If the above-mentioned water changes in taste, odor, or color because of impure contacts,

---

*About 70 centimeters or 27 inches.
†About 390 kilograms or 860 pounds.

such as with blood or urine, it becomes impure; but if it indirectly changes in odor, color, or taste because of some impure matter, for example if its odor is changed because of the proximity of some decomposing matter, it remains pure.

*   *   *   *

Water which has been polluted by blood, urine, or other impurities, and has thereby been changed in odor, color, or taste, is purified by running water or by rainwater which falls directly into it, or rainwater driven into it by the wind, or carried to it by a drainpipe, and thereby regains its purifying properties.

*   *   *   *

That a quantity of water is enough to be purifying may be established in one of two ways: either through one's own personal conviction that it is, or by two trustworthy men affirming that it is.

*   *   *   *

The water used for washing the urinary orifice and the anus remains pure in five cases: if it has neither the odor, the color, nor the taste of urine or feces; if no external impurity has touched it; if no other impure matter such as blood issued from the anus or the urinary orifice at the same time as the excrement or urine; if no particles of excrement or urine are visible in the water; if the excrement that touched the anus was not exceptionally abundant.

❊ ❊ ❊ ❊

Running water, even though in lesser quantity than that of purifying water, remains pure and therefore drinkable if it contains excrement or urine, provided however that the admixture of these has not altered its odor, color, or taste.

❊ ❊ ❊ ❊

If excrement, urine, or other impurities have polluted running water, only that part of it which has been changed in odor, color, or taste becomes impure; the rest remains pure.

❊ ❊ ❊ ❊

If excrement, urine, or any other impurity should be on the roof of a house and be rained upon, the rainwater remains pure if it continues falling and running directly off the roof or down a gutter or drainpipe; but if the rain stops, the water that continues running off and which is known to have touched the impurities on the roof is impure.

14

On Ablution*

There are two kinds of ablutions: the kind known as "step by step," which consists of washing the different parts of the body one after the other, and the kind known as "total," in which the whole body is immersed in water.

＊ ＊ ＊ ＊

In step-by-step ablutions, one must begin by proclaiming in both a loud and a low voice that one is planning to perform his ablutions; after that, one should wash one's head and the back of the neck, then the right side of the body, followed by the left side. If this precise order is not followed, whether deliberately or out of ignorance, the ablutions are not valid. It

---

*Ablution is the indispensable ritual which consists of purifying one's body when it has been soiled by an impurity, whether external or originating within the body (as indicated later). This ritual must be carried out.

is to be pointed out that the right side of the navel and the right side of the genitals must be washed with the right side of the body, and the left side of the navel and genitals with the left side of the body. However, it is more prudent to wash navel and genitals in their entirety along with each side of the body. If, once the ablution is completed, one suspects that some part of the body has been overlooked, the ritual must be repeated; in that case, if the overlooked part is on the left side of the body, it is enough to wash only that part, but if it is on the right side of the body, after washing that part, the whole left side of the body must be washed again.

* * * *

In a total ablution, one must immerse the entire body in water, after having proclaimed in both a loud and a low voice that this is one's intention. If one notices, after the ablution, that some part of the body remained outside the water, even though one may not know exactly which part of the body it was, the entire ritual must be repeated.

* * * *

It is necessary that during ablution not one part of the body remain unwashed; however, it is not required that one wash those parts which are not visible, such as the inside of the ears or nose. In the case of ears that are

pierced, the holes in them must be washed if
they are large enough so the insides of them
can be seen; otherwise, this is not necessary.

* * * *

During ablution, one must wash the short-
est hairs on the body, but it is recommended
that even the longest be washed. If one washes
his anus in the water of a public bath, one must
first obtain the permission of the owner of this
bath for the ablution to be valid. If, during
ablution, one breaks wind or urinates, the ritual
remains valid. If one performs his ablutions
after having ejaculated and one has a verse of
the Koran or the name of God written or tat-
tooed on his body, one's hand must not touch
that part of the body during the ablution, but
that part must be washed without being
touched.

* * * *

Sperm is always impure, whether it results from actual coitus or from an emission
while one is either conscious or asleep, whether
it is abundant or not, whether or not it results
from sexual pleasure, whether emission is in-
tentional or not.

* * * *

It is recommended that one urinate after
ejaculation; if one does not, the discharge that

might follow one's ablution would have to be considered to be sperm, even though it seems doubtful.

✻ ✻ ✻ ✻

During sexual intercourse, if the penis enters a woman's vagina or a man's anus, fully or only as far as the circumcision ring, both partners become impure, even if they have not reached puberty; they must consequently perform their ablutions.

✻ ✻ ✻ ✻

If the man thinks that he has not entered the woman's vagina beyond the circumcision ring, ablution is not required.

✻ ✻ ✻ ✻

If a man—God protect him from it!— fornicates with an animal and ejaculates, ablution is necessary.

✻ ✻ ✻ ✻

If the sperm moves inside the penis but does not come out, or if there is doubt about whether it actually was emitted, ablution is not required.

✻ ✻ ✻ ✻

A man who has ejaculated and has not yet performed his ablutions must avoid the follow-

ing ten acts: eating; drinking; reading more
than seven verses of the Koran; touching the
binding of the Koran, or the margins of its
pages, or the spaces between the lines; carrying the Koran on his person; sleeping; dyeing
his beard with henna; anointing himself with
grease or oil; having sexual intercourse after
having ejaculated in his sleep.

* * * *

If a man has sexual intercourse with his
wife during the periods of prescribed abstinence, such as the month's fast of Ramadan,
his sweat is impure and he may not say his
daily prayers while in such a state.

* * * *

If a man becomes aroused by a woman
other than his wife but then has intercourse
with his own wife, it is preferable for him not
to pray if he has sweated; but if he first has
intercourse with his spouse and then with another woman, he may say his prayers even
though he be in a sweat.

* * * *

A man who has ejaculated as a result of intercourse with a woman other than his wife,
and who then ejaculates again while having
coitus with his legal wife, does not have the
right to say his prayers while still sweating; but

if he has had intercourse with his wife first and then with a woman not his wife, he may say his prayers even though still sweating.

* * * *

If a fly or any other insect settled first on something impure that is moist and then on so thing pure that is moist, the latter in turn becomes impure, provided one can be certain that the former was impure; failing that, it remains pure.

* * * *

Besides the ablutions that are necessary and unavoidable there are a number of ablutions that are highly recommended in order to please God. A few of them are:

Ablution performed Friday between dawn and noon.

Ablution performed on the eve of the first day of Ramadan and the eves of all the odd days of that month, (third, fifth, seventh, and so on). The ablutions on the eves of the first, fifteenth, seventeenth, nineteenth, twenty-first, twenty-third, twenty-fifth, twenty-seventh, and twenty-ninth days of Ramadan are especially recommended. On the eve of the twenty-third day, one would be well advised to perform two ablutions, one at the beginning and the other at the end of the night.

Ablution performed by a woman who has used perfume for a man other than her husband.

On Ablution

Ablution of the man who has fallen asleep while in a drunken state.

Ablution of a man or woman who, during a total eclipse of the sun or the moon, have not said their prayers.

Ablution of one who has witnessed the hanging of a person condemned to death. If he did not witness it of his own free will, ablution is not necessarily required.

15

On the Five Namaz*

The person who says his five daily prayers must do so in a state of perfect concentration and complete meditation. He must abstain from committing sins such as those of jealousy, pride, or scandalmongering, or eating forbidden foods, drinking alcoholic beverages, or refusing to pay his tithes to the clergy. It is also preferable that he abstain from committing such venial sins as saying his daily prayers while half asleep or holding back his need to urinate, nor should he look up at the sky while praying. On the other hand, he would do well before praying to make sure that he has agate rings on his fingers, that he is properly dressed and well combed, that his teeth are brushed, and that he is perfumed.

---

*A *namaz* is an Islamic ritual or prayer which every Moslem must perform five times a day: at dawn, at noon, at midafternoon, at dusk, and after it has become dark.

❋ ❋ ❋ ❋

While he is performing his five daily prayers, a man must make sure that, even if they cannot be seen, his genitals and his rear are covered. It is better if he covers the whole part of his body from the navel to the knees.

❋ ❋ ❋ ❋

A woman, while saying her five daily prayers, must cover her entire body, including her head and her hair; however, it is permissible for her to leave uncovered a part of her face and hands and her feet up to the ankles.

❋ ❋ ❋ ❋

If a man should discover, while saying his prayer, that his member is not covered, he must cover it immediately, and if that takes too much time, he must stop his prayer and start over from the beginning. But if he discovers that his member is not covered only after completing his prayer, the prayer remains valid.

❋ ❋ ❋ ❋

During daily prayer, it is permissible to cover one's body and genitals with grass or the leaves of trees, but it is better to do this only when there are no other means at hand.

❋ ❋ ❋ ❋

During joint prayer, the woman must position herself behind the man. If the woman and the man enter the place of worship at the same time and the woman happens to find herself in front of the man, she must say her prayer again after placing herself where she belongs, i.e., behind the man.

❋ ❋ ❋ ❋

It is highly recommended to avoid eating at the same table as one who does not attend the mosque; one must also avoid asking the advice of such a one, living near him, marrying a woman of his family, or giving him one's daughter in marriage.

❋ ❋ ❋ ❋

It is forbidden to say one's daily prayers in the following places: a bath; saline ground; facing someone else; facing an open door; on a highway, an avenue, or a street; before a fireplace or lamp; in the kitchen and any other place where there is an oven; in front of a well or cesspool; facing a portrait or statue of a living model, unless these are covered; in the presence of someone who has ejaculated and has not yet performed his ablutions; in a room it which there is a photograph, even if it is not located facing the person praying; facing a grave, or on a grave, or between two graves, in a cemetery.

* * * *

It is not advisable to allow a feebleminded person, a child, or someone who has just eaten garlic into the mosque.

* * * *

One who falls asleep while saying his prayer must say it over again if he realizes he dozed during the prayer; if he is not sure of having done so, the prayer remains valid.

* * * *

Coughing, belching loudly, or sighing does not invalidate a prayer. On the other hand, the prayer is voided if one emits interjections of two letters or more.

* * * *

If a person who is praying turns red in the face from suppressing an impulse to burst out laughing, that person must start the prayer over again.

* * * *

If a person sobs aloud while praying because of some earthly sorrow, the prayer is invalid; but if he weeps to himself, the prayer is valid. However, if it is not over an earthly sorrow but because of the fear of God or the hereafter, he is urgently encouraged to weep.

❊ ❊ ❊ ❊

Clapping one's hands or jumping up in the air during a prayer makes it null and void.

❊ ❊ ❊ ❊

If, during prayer, one swallows bits of food left over between one's teeth, the prayer is not invalidated; but if one has a piece of sugar in his mouth and the sugar slowly melts during the prayer, the value of the latter is debatable.

❊ ❊ ❊ ❊

During prayer, one must avoid bending one's head to the right or left, closing one's eyes, clasping one's hands, spitting, toying with one's beard, looking at the writings of the Koran or any other writings, or at the design of a ring. One must also avoid praying when one feels sleepy, when one feels an urge to urinate or defecate, or when one is wearing socks that are too tight.

16

On Prayers in Case of Natural Phenomena

Namazé-ayat is the name given to the prayer to be said when one witnesses natural phenomena which inspire fear. This prayer is required in the four following cases: total or partial eclipse of the sun; total or partial eclipse of the moon; earthquake, even though it be not fearsome; thunder, lightning, and black or red winds.

❋ ❋ ❋ ❋

If several of these phenomena occur simultaneously, for instance if an eclipse should be accompanied by an earthquake, two prayers are required.

❋ ❋ ❋ ❋

In case of earthquake or lighting or thunder, one must pray immediately. Failing to do so is a sin which is not pardoned until after this prayer is said, no matter how much later, even to the last day of a person's life.

* * * *

If a woman is having her period during a solar or lunar eclipse and until the eclipse is over, no prayer for this natural phenomenon is required. Nor is she obliged to say it at a later date.

17

On Fasting

Sexual intercourse is a breaking of the fast, even if the penis enters the vagina only as far as the circumcision ring, and even if no ejaculation results.

❊ ❊ ❊ ❊

If the penis enters less deeply into the vagina and there is no ejaculation, the fast has not been broken.

❊ ❊ ❊ ❊

If the man cannot determine with certainty what length of his penis entered into the vagina, and if he has gone in beyond the circumcision ring, his fast has not been broken.

❊ ❊ ❊ ❊

If a man has intercourse because he has forgotten that he is in a fasting period, or if someone forces him to have intercourse, his fast has not been broken. But if he remembers the fast while the sex act is taking place, or if he is no longer forcibly constrained to complete the coitus, he must interrupt it immediately.

* * * *

If a man during a fasting period masturbates and brings himself to ejaculation, his fast has been broken.

* * * *

If a man ejaculates involuntarily, his fast remains valid, but if he himself does anything whatsoever to help along his involuntary ejaculation, the fast is considered to be null and void.

* * * *

Taking an enema, even for medically therapeutic reasons, breaks the fast; but the use of suppositories is not forbidden; however, it is preferable to abstain from using opium suppositories.

* * * *

The fast of one who, in thought, or word, or deed, bears false witness against God, or His Prophet or his successors, is immediately invalidated, even though he may confess on the spot to having lied and proclaim his repentance. In all likelihood, Saint Fatima [the daughter of Mohammed and wife of Ali], as well as the other prophets and their successors, are also included among those against whom one may not blaspheme.

* * * *

If, during the fast, one attributes in all good faith some statement to God or to His Prophet, and one afterward learns that his was in error, the fast remains valid. If one intentionally attributes some false quotation to God or to His Prophet or his successors, the fast loses its value; but if one is only repeating such a quotation heard from a third party, the fast remains valid.

* * * *

The fast is invalidated if one plunges his entire head under water, but if one immerses only the right side and then the left side, the value of the fast remains intact. One's head must not be immersed in rose water; however, it may be immersed in other waters in solution, or in other liquids.

* * * *

If, in order to rescue a person from drowning, one's head becomes immersed during a period of fasting, one's fast is invalidated, even if there was no other way of saving the drowning person's life.

* * * *

If one has ejaculated and abstains from performing the prescribed ablutions during the vigil of the month of Ramadan, the fast loses its value.

* * * *

If a person believes he will have sufficient time, before a Ramadan vigil, to complete his ablutions after ejaculation, but discovers afterward that he does not have time enough, he may postpone his ablutions in order to begin the fast.

* * * *

If a fly enters the mouth of a person during a period of fasting, he is not forced to take it out, if it has not gone too far into the throat; if it has remained in the mouth, he must take it out even if that causes vomiting which invalidates the fast.

* * * *

If by inadvertence one eats something during the fast, and one then realizes it, one must not attempt to retrieve the part of it which has already been swallowed.

* * * *

The following practices are inadvisable during fasts: putting drops in one's eyes; having a blood transfusion or taking a bath; pinching snuff or smelling aromatic plants; taking sitz baths (applies to women only); taking suppositories; getting one's clothes wet; having teeth pulled or undergoing any other surgery which might cause blood to flow into the mouth; brushing one's teeth with a moist wood; becoming intimate with one's wife, even without the intention of coming to ejaculation, or deliberately arousing oneself (if ejaculation is deliberately brought about, the fast is invalidated).

18

On Woman and Her Periods

<hr>

Woman is pseudo-menstrual when blood is discharged from her vagina outside the time of her regular periods. The blood may be yellowish, cold, and fluid, and be discharged without any burning sensation; it may also be blackish or yellow, hot, thick, and cause a burning sensation as is passes.

✤ ✤ ✤ ✤

Pseudo-menses are of three kinds: weak, medium, and abundant. If the blood does not fully soak a piece of cotton introduced into the vagina, the pseudo-menses are weak; if it soaks the cotton without going through to the fabric placed over the vulva, the pseudo-menses are medium; if, on the other hand, the blood soaks through both cotton and fabric, these are abundant pseudo-menses.

❃ ❃ ❃ ❃

In the case of weak pseudo-menses, the woman must wash according to religious ritual before praying, change the cotton or wash it, and also wash her vulva if it has been soiled by the blood.

❃ ❃ ❃ ❃

The menstrual period proper is the period of those few days during the month when blood is discharged from women's vaginas. This blood is most often thick, hot, blackish red or bright red, and gushes forth with a burning sensation.

❃ ❃ ❃ ❃

Women of the lineage of the Prophet of Islam are menopausal at the age of sixty; others, once they are over fifty.

❃ ❃ ❃ ❃

Blood that is discharged from the vagina of a girl under the age of nine and a woman over the age of sixty can therefore not be considered menstrual blood.

❃ ❃ ❃ ❃

The pregnant woman and the nursing woman may have regular menstrual periods.

＊　＊　＊　＊

It is indispensable that during the first three days of the menses, the blood not be stopped from flowing; therefore, if the flow ceases after two days to resume a day later, it is not menstrual blood.

＊　＊　＊　＊

It is not indispensable that the blood flow out of the vagina for all of the three days; it is sufficient that there be some inside the vagina.

＊　＊　＊　＊

If a woman sees blood flowing from her vagina for more than three days and less than ten days, and is not sure whether this is menstrual blood or blood from an abscess, she must attempt to introduce a piece of cotton into her vagina and then withdraw it. If the blood runs out on the left side, it is menstrual blood; if on the right side, it is from an abscess.

＊　＊　＊　＊

If a woman sees blood flowing from her vagina and wonders whether it is menstrual blood or the blood of her hymen, she must introduce a piece of cotton into her vagina and leave it there for a while before withdrawing it. If the blood has spotted only the edges of the cotton, it is the blood of the hymen; if the whole piece of cotton is soaked with blood, it is menstrual.

* * * *

If a woman sees blood flow from her vagina for less than three days, then stop and resume for a period of three days, it is this second flow which must be considered to be that of the menses, even if the first one coincided more exactly with her menstrual cycle.

* * * *

During the time a woman is menstruating, it is preferable for a man to avoid coitus, even if it does not involve full pentration—that is, as far as the circumcision ring—and even if it does not involve ejaculation. It is also highly inadvisable for him to sodomize her during this time.

* * * *

If the number of days of the woman's menstrual period is divided by three, a husband who has intercourse with her during the first two days must pay the equivalent of 18 *nokhods** of gold to the poor; if he has it on the third or fourth days, the equivalent of 9 *nokhods;* and if he has it during the last two days, the equivalent of 4½ *nokhods.*

---

*About 3 grams or 1/10 ounce.

* * * *

Sodomizing a menstruating woman does not require such payment.

* * * *

If a man has intercourse with his wife during all three of these periods, he must pay the equivalent in gold of 3½ *nokhods*. If the price of gold has changed between the time of the coitus and the time of payment, the rate in effect on the date of payment will prevail.

* * * *

If during an act of intercourse a man notices that the woman has begun menstruating, he must withdraw; if he fails to, he must give alms to the poor.

* * * *

If such a man cannot afford to give alms to the poor, he must at least give something to a beggar. If he cannot afford that either, he must ask forgiveness of God.

* * * *

After a wife's menstrual period, her husband may repudiate her, even if she has not yet made her ablutions. He may also indulge in relations with her, but it is preferable that he wait until she has made her ablutions. In the interim, the woman is not authorized to do anything which is forbidden to her during menstruation, such as going into a mosque or touching the writing of the Koran, until she has completed her ablutions.

19

On Marriage, Adultery, and Conjugal Relations

A woman may legally belong to a man in one of two ways; by continuing marriage or temporary marriage. In the former, the duration of the marriage need not be specified; in the latter, it must be stipulated, for example, that it is for a period of an hour, a day, a month, a year, or more.

❖   ❖   ❖   ❖

Marriage, whether continuing or temporary, must be sealed by a religious formula spoken either by the woman or by the man, or by one of their representatives.

❖   ❖   ❖   ❖

As long as the woman and man have not contracted a religious marriage, they are not

entitled to look upon one another. To allow
that, it is not enough to assume that the marriage formula has been spoken, but if the person representing them states that it has been
spoken, then that is enough to validate the
marriage.

✳ ✳ ✳ ✳

If a woman authorizes someone to marry
her to a man for a period of ten days, for
example, without specifying the exact date, the
man may contract the marriage at his pleasure,
but if the woman has specified a precise day
and hour, the formula must be spoken at that
specified time.

✳ ✳ ✳ ✳

The legal marriage formula must be read
in Arabic, but if one cannot speak that language correctly, it may be spoken in a different
language.

✳ ✳ ✳ ✳

A father or a paternal grandfather his the
right to marry off a child who is insane or has
not reached puberty by acting as its representative. The child may not annul such a marriage after reaching puberty or regaining his
sanity, unless the marriage is to his manifest
disadvantage.

❋ ❋ ❋ ❋

Any girl who is of age, that is, capable of understanding what is in her own best interest, if she wishes to get married and is a virgin, must procure the authorization of her father or paternal grandfather. The permission of her mother or brother is not required.

❋ ❋ ❋ ❋

If a father or paternal grandfather marries off prepubic son or grandson, the latter will be responsible once he has reached puberty, for taking care of his wife's material needs.

❋ ❋ ❋ ❋

A marriage is annulled if a man finds that his wife is afflicted with one of the seven following debilities: madness, leprosy, eczema, blindness, paralysis with aftereffects, malformation of the urinary and genital tracts or of the genital tract and rectum through conjoining thereof, or vaginal malformation making coitus impossible.

❋ ❋ ❋ ❋

If a wife finds out after marriage that her husband is suffering from mental illness, that he is a castrate, impotent, or has had his testicles excised, she may apply for annulment of her marriage.

* * * *

If a wife has her marriage annulled because her husband is unable to have sexual relations with her either vaginally or anally, he must pay her as damages one-half of the dowry specified in the marriage contract. If the husband or wife annuls the marriage for any of the above-mentioned reasons, the man owes nothing to the woman if they have had sexual relations together; if they have not, he must pay her the full amount of the dowry.

* * * *

It is forbidden to marry one's mother, sister, or stepmother.

* * * *

It is forbidden to marry's one's mother-in-law, or one's wife's maternal or paternal grandmothers or any of her great-grandmothers, even though one's marriage to her may never have been consummated.

* * * *

A man who marries a woman and has sexual relations with her may not marry her daughter or granddaughter, even if these be by a different marriage.

97

* * * *

A man may not marry his wife's daughter, even if their marriage has not been consummated.

* * * *

Aunts of the bride's father and the aunts of her grandparents need not wear the veil in the presence of the groom; the father, grandfather, and great-grandfather of the groom, as well as his sons, grandsons, and all his male descendants, may freely look upon the bride.

* * * *

A man may not marry the nieces of his wife without the latter's consent; if he should nevertheless do so without getting consent, but his wife raises no objection, then there is no problem.

* * * *

A man who has committed adultery with his aunt must not marry her daughters, that is to say, his first cousins.

* * * *

If a man who has married his first cousin commits adultery with her mother, the marriage is not thereby annulled.

❈ ❈ ❈ ❈

If a man commits adultery with a woman other than his aunt, it is highly recommended that he not marry the daughter of that woman. If he marries a woman, consummates the marriage, and then commits adultery with her mother, the marriage is not thereby annulled. Nor is it automatically annulled in the case of his having committed such adultery before the marriage was consummated, but in that case it is better if the husband voluntarily annuls the marriage.

❈ ❈ ❈ ❈

A Moslem woman may not marry a non-Moslem man; nor may a Moslem man marry a non-Moslem woman in continuing marriage, but he may take a Jewish or Christian woman in temporary marriage.

❈ ❈ ❈ ❈

A man who marries an already married woman must break off his marriage with her and refrain from ever marrying her again.

❈ ❈ ❈ ❈

A married woman remains legally married after having committed adultery; however, should she not repent and should she continue to be unfaithful to her husband, it is preferable for the latter to repudiate her, but with full payment to her of her dowry.

* * * *

The mother, sister, or daughter of a man who has been sodomized by another man may not marry the latter, even if both men or one of them had not yet reached puberty at the time; but if the one who was the victim of the act cannot prove it, his mother, sister, or daughter is allowed to marry the other man.

* * * *

If a man who has married a girl who has not reached puberty possesses her sexually before her ninth birthday, inflicting traumatisms upon her, he has no right to repeat such an act with her.

* * * *

If a man sodomizes the son, brother, or father of his wife after their marriage, the marriage remains valid.

* * * *

A woman who has contracted a continuing marriage does not have the right to go out of the house without her husband's permission;

she must remain at his disposal for the fulfillment of any one of his desires, and may not refuse herself to him except for a religiously valid reason. If she is totally submissive to him, the husband must provide her with her food, clothing, and lodging, whether or not he has the means to do so.

❋ ❋ ❋ ❋

A woman who refuses herself to her husband is guilty, and may not demand from him food, clothing, lodging, or any later sexual relations; however, she retains the right to be paid damages if she is repudiated.

❋ ❋ ❋ ❋

A husband is not obligated to pay any travel expenses incurred by his wife which exceed what her expenses would have been at home; but if the travel was undertaken at his own suggestion, then he must take care of the expenses.

❋ ❋ ❋ ❋

A wife who scrupuluously obeys her husband has the right to be paid the daily household expenses for any of the husband's assets, in the case the latter refuses voluntarily to pay for them. But if she is forced to meet such expenses out of her own pocket, she is not obligated to obey her husband.

* * * *

A man who has contracted a continuing marriage may not leave his wife for so long a time as to allow her to question the validity of the marriage; however, he is not obligated to spend one night out of every four with her.

* * * *

A husband must have sexual relations with his wife at least once in every four months.

* * * *

If, at the time of contracting the marriage, no specific time was indicated at which the husband was to pay the dowry to his wife, the wife may refuse herself to her husband for so long as that amount of money has not been paid her.

But once she has agreed to have sexual relations with her husband, she can no longer later refuse to, except for religiously valid reasons.

* * * *

A temporary marriage, even though only one of convenience, is nevertheless legal.

❈ ❈ ❈ ❈

A man must not abstain from having sexual relations with his temporary wife for more than four months.

❈ ❈ ❈ ❈

If the temporary marriage contract includes a clause specifying that the husband is not entitled to have normal sexual relations with his wife, such a clause must be respected. He must then be satisfied with giving her pleasures in other ways. But as soon as the wife consents to it, he may perform the natural sex act with her.

❈ ❈ ❈ ❈

A woman who has been temporarily married in exchange for a previously established dowry has no right to demand that her daily expenses be paid by her husband, even when she becomes pregnant.

❈ ❈ ❈ ❈

A temporarily married wife may not inherit from her husband; nor may he inherit from her.

❈ ❈ ❈ ❈

A temporarily married woman is entitled to go out of the house without asking her husband's permission, unless the fact of her so going out harms him in one way or another.

* * * *

If a father (or paternal grandfather) marries off his daughter (or granddaughter) in her absence without knowing for a certainty that she is alive, the marriage becomes null and void as soon as it is established that she was dead at the time of the marriage.

* * * *

It is forbidden for a man to look upon the body of a woman who is not his wife, under any pretext whatsoever. It is equally forbidden for a woman to look upon the body of a man who is not her husband.

* * * *

To look upon the face and hair of a girl who has not reached puberty, if it is done without intention of enjoyment thereof, and if one is not afraid of succumbing to temptation, may be tolerated. It is however recommended that one not look upon her belly or thighs, which must remain covered.

* * * *

To look upon the faces and hands of Jewish or Christian women, if this is not done with intention of enjoyment thereof, and if one does not fear temptation, is tolerated.

❊ ❊ ❊ ❊

A woman must hide her body and her hair from the eyes of men. It is highly recommended that she also hide them from those of prepubic boys, if she suspects that they may look upon her with lust.

❊ ❊ ❊ ❊

It is forbidden to look upon the genitals of another person, even from behind a glass, or in a mirror, or in standing water. It is even expressly recommended to abstain from looking at the genitals of a child who knows the difference between good and evil. But it is permitted for husband and wife to look upon each other in all parts of their bodies.

❊ ❊ ❊ ❊

A man must not look upon the body of another man with lustful intent. Likewise, a woman may not look upon another woman with such intent.

❊ ❊ ❊ ❊

It is not forbidden for a man to photograph a woman other than his wife, but if in

105

order to do so he must touch her, then he must
not photograph her.

* * * *

If a woman is called upon to give an enema
to a woman or to a man other than her husband, or to wash their genitals, then she must
cover her hand so as not to come into direct
contact with the genital organs; the same pre-
cautions must be taken by a man where another man or a woman other than his wife are
concerned.

* * * *

If a man is called upon, for medical reasons, to look upon a woman other than his wife
and to touch her body, he is permitted to do so,
but if he can give such care by only looking at
the body he must not touch it, and if he can
give it by only touching, he must not look at
it.

* * * *

If a man or woman be forced, in order to
administer medical care, to look upon the genitals of another person, he or she must do so
indirectly, in a mirror, except in case of absolute necessity.

* * * *

If the husband has included in the marriage contract a clause guaranteeing his wife's

virginity, he may annul the marriage if it turns
out that she was not a virgin.

* * * *

If a woman abjures her faith before her
marriage is consummated, the marriage is annulled; the like is true after conclusion of the
marriage, if she is menopausal. But if she is
not menopausal and returns to her Moslem beliefs within a hundred days after the breaking
off of the marriage, it again becomes valid.

* * * *

A man whose father or mother was a Moslem at the time of his conception, and who
himself embraced the Moslem faith after
reaching puberty, will have his marriage automatically abolished if he becomes an apostate.

* * * *

The marriage of a man born of non-
Moslem parents but who himself became a convert to Islam is automatically annulled if he
renounces his faith before consummating the
marriage. If he renounces his faith after having sexual relations with his wife, she must
wait one hundred days after the annulment of
the marriage before marrying again, if she is
of an age to have menstrual periods. Thus, the
marriage remains valid if during those one
hundred days the husband returns to the Moslem fold; otherwise, the annulment is irrever-
sible.

✤ ✤ ✤ ✤

If the woman inserts into the marriage contract a cause binding her husband not to move her away from the city, and the husband accepts such a clause, then he must abide by it.

✤ ✤ ✤ ✤

The husband of a woman who has had a daughter by a previous marriage may marry that daughter to a son of his by a previous marriage. He himself has the right to marry the mother of a girl married to his son.

✤ ✤ ✤ ✤

A woman who becomes pregnant as a result of adultery must not have an abortion.

✤ ✤ ✤ ✤

If a man commits adultery with an unmarried woman, and subsequently marries her, the child born of that marriage will be a bastard unless the parents can be sure it was conceived after they were married.

✤ ✤ ✤ ✤

One need not believe a woman who claims to have entered menopause. On the one hand, she must be belived if she asserts that she is not married.

* * * *

It is highly recommended that a girl be married off as soon as she reaches the age of puberty. One of the blessings of man is to have his daughter experience her first period not in her father's house, but in that of her husband.

* * * *

A child born of an adulterous father is legitimate.

* * * *

It is a sin to have sexual relations with one's wife during the fast of Ramadan or while she is having her menses, but the child born of such relations is legitimate.

* * * *

If a man marries a woman and possesses her sexually, he may no longer marry any girl whom this woman has breast-fed.

* * * *

A man may not marry a wet nurse who has breast-fed his wife.

109

* * * *

A man may not marry a girl who was ever breast-fed by his mother or his grandmother.

* * * *

The best person to breast-feed a newborn baby it its own mother. It is preferable that she not ask to be paid for such service, but that her husband pay her for it of his own free will. If the sum the mother asks for is greater than that charged by a wet nurse, the husband is free to take the child from its mother and turn it over to the wet nurse.

* * * *

It is recommended that the wet nurse be a faithful Shi'ite, intelligent, modest, and pretty. On the other hand, it is most inadvisable that she be feebleminded, a nonbeliever in the Twelve Imams, ugly, or a bastard, or of bad character. It is equally inadvisable to select as wet nurse a woman who has an illegitimate child.

* * * *

It is recommended that every child be breast-fed for two whole years.

20

On Divorce

A man who repudiates his wife must be of sound mind and past the age of puberty. He must do so of his own free will and without any constraint; therefore, if the formula for divorce is spoken in jest the marriage is not annulled.

❊　❊　❊　❊

The woman must not be having her period at the time of the divorce, and the husband must not have had sexual relations with her since her last period.

❊　❊　❊　❊

In three cases, a man may repudiate his wife while she is having her period: if he has had no sexual relations with her since their marriage; if she is pregnant while the husband believes she is having her period, and it is learned only later that she was pregnant at the time of the repudiation; if he is not certain, because of the distance that separates them, whether his wife is then having her period.

* * * *

A man who has had sexual relations with his wife after her last menstrual period must wait for her to have her next one before he may divorce her. But he may divorce his wife if she has not yet reached her ninth birthday, or is pregnant, or is menopausal.

* * * *

If a husband who has had sexual relations with his wife between menstrual periods, divorces her during this time and learns later that she was pregnant when the divorce took place, the latter remains valid.

* * * *

A woman temporarily married, say, for a month or a year, has her marriage automatically annulled at the end of that time, or at any other time when the husband releases her from the balance of her engagement. It is not necessary for this that there be any witnesses, or that the woman have had her period.

❖ ❖ ❖ ❖

A woman who has not yet reached the age of nine or a menopausal woman may remarry immediately after divorce, without waiting the hundred days that are otherwise required.

❖ ❖ ❖ ❖

A woman who has had her ninth birthday, or who has not yet entered menopause, must wait for three menstrual periods after her divorce before being allowed to remarry.

❖ ❖ ❖ ❖

If a woman who has not reached her ninth birthday or who has not entered menopause gets temporarily married, she must, at the end of the contract or when the husband has released her from part of it, wait two menstrual periods or forty-five days before marrying again.

❖ ❖ ❖ ❖

If a man commits adultery with a woman he knows is not his wife, while the woman is unaware that the man is not her husband, she must wait one hundred days before remarrying.

If a man encourages a married woman to leave her husband so as to marry him, they are both committing a great sin, but the divorce and their marriage remain in force.

* * * *

If the father or paternal grandfather of a boy has him marry a woman for a temporary marriage, he may prematurely cancel it in the boy's interest, even if the marriage was contracted before the boy reached the age of puberty. If, for example, a fourteen-year-old boy has been married off to a woman for a period of two years, they may return her freedom to the woman before this time has run its course; but a continuing marriage cannot be broken in this way.

* * * *

If a man repudiates his wife without informing her of it, and continues to meet her expenses for a period of, say, a year, and at the end of that time informs her that he got a divorce a year earlier and shows her proof of it, he may require that she return to him anything he has bought or given her during that time, provided that she has not used it up or consumed it, in which case he cannot demand its return.

21

On the Mortuary Ritual

If a part of the body becomes detached, whether after or before death, and one touches such a part when the cleansing of the corpse has not yet been completed, one must undergo a purifying ablution; but this it not necessary if the part of the body involved is boneless.

* * * *

If one touches a bone or a tooth removed from a corpse, ablution is necessary; but it is not required if the bone or tooth was removed from a live body, unless there is a muscle attached to it.

One must avoid leaving a dying person alone, placing a heavy object on his belly, leaving him the care of a man who has ejaculated or a woman who is having her period, speaking too much in his presence, weeping, or leaving him in the sole care of women.

* * * *

Ablution of a dead man by a woman, or vice versa, is forbidden. But the woman may perform this ritual if the man is her husband, and the man in the case of his own wife. However, it is preferable that they do not do it.

* * * *

It is forbidden to look upon the sexual organs of a dead man or woman. The person performing the ablution ritual commits a cardinal sin if he violates this ban, but the ablution does not thereby lose its validity.

* * * *

During the ritual, the genitals of the corpse must remain covered, even if only by a piece of wood or a brick.

* * * *

If a person dies in a well and it is impossible to get the body out, the well must be shut off and become his tomb.

* * * *

If a child dies within the mother's womb and it is a danger to her life to leave it there, it must be extracted in the easiest way possible; it can, if need be, be cut into pieces; this should be done either by the woman's husband or by a woman of this profession.

✤ ✤ ✤ ✤

One has no right to exhume the body of a Moslem, not even that of a child or of a madman, unless it has turned to dust.

✤ ✤ ✤ ✤

One may exhume a body if it is done in order to remove a still living child from its mother's womb, or if there is danger that a wild animal may devour it, or that a flood may carry it away, or that it may fall into the hands of the enemy. One may also reopen a sepulcher in order to deposit in it a part of the departed one's body which has been found or recovered after the burial.

22

On Finance and Taxes

All commercial transactions which involve any of the following are declared null and void: trade in urine, excrement, or alcoholic beverages; trade in misappropriated wealth, unless the owner thereof agrees to it; trade in anything other than merchandise; trade in musical instruments or gambling accessories; trade based upon interest produced by a sum of money; sale of any adulterated merchandise, unless the buyer is informed of the fact in advance.

* * * *

Trade in oil, curative solutions, and perfumes imported from non-Moslem countries is allowed, provided that their impurity has not been proven; on the other hand, fat is impure if it is produced in an Islamic country and comes from an animal which has not been established to have been slaughtered according to Moslem ritual. Trade in such products is illegal.

❋ ❋ ❋ ❋

There can be no trade in skins of foxes which died or were slaughtered in manners contrary to Moslem ritual.

❋ ❋ ❋ ❋

Trade in meat, fat, and skins is allowed, provided the seller is a Moslem; but it is forbidden if the buyer knows that this Moslem got them from an infidel, unless it is formally established that the animals were killed in accordance with the rules prevailing in Islam.

❋ ❋ ❋ ❋

Any trade in objects for enjoyment, such as musical instruments, however small they may be, is strictly illegal.

❋ ❋ ❋ ❋

A Moslem is allowed to require payment by an infidel of interest on money that he has lent him. This is also allowed between father and child, and between husband and wife.

❋ ❋ ❋ ❋

Persons who work oil deposits, or gold, silver, lead, copper, iron, turquoise, salt or other mines must pay the *khoms* [tax equivalent to one-fifth of income] to the Islamic Treasury provided the income therefrom reaches the required minimum. This minimum must be the equivalent in value of coins comprising 415 grams of silver or 45 grams of gold, after deduction of expenses. If the income does not reach such a figure, the *khoms* is still due if the gross income exceeds annual expenses.

* * * *

Anyone who discovers a treasure the value of which is at least that of coins of 415 grams of silver or 45 grams of gold must also pay the *khoms* to the Islamic Treasury.

* * * *

If a person buys an animal and thereafter discovers in its belly some valuable object, he must first inquire of the seller whether that object belongs to him. If it does not, he must check back with previous owners. If it turns out that the object belongs to none of them, he must pay the *khoms*, even if the price of the object is less than that of 415 grams of silver or 45 grams of gold.

* * * *

If someone dives into a river, such as the Tigris or the Euphrates, and comes up with a jewel, he must pay the *khoms* on its value, provided that such rivers are known customarily to contain such jewels.

* * * *

If a person dives and comes up with a quantity of amber of value in excess of 4 grams of gold, he must pay the *khoms* on it, even if it was the result of more than single dive.

* * * *

If a child discovers a mine or a treasure or finds a jewel under water, his father or guardian must pay the *khoms* on it.

* * * *

The income from the *khoms* collected throughout the country is to be divided between and *Seyed* [descendants of the Prophet] and the Holy Imam, represented in our time by a *Modjtahed* [learned man]. The *Seyed*'s share is to be meted out, with the *Modjtahed*'s permission, to poor *Seyed*, orphaned *Seyed*, and ruined *Seyed*. The Imam's share may be spent only with the permission of his representative on earth, the *Modjtahed*.

* * * *

The *zakat* [legal contribution or tithe] for camels is to be computed on the basis of twelve brackets:

one sheep for five camels;
two sheep for ten camels;
three sheep for fifteen camels;

four sheep for twenty camels;

five sheep for twenty-five camels;

one second-year camel for twenty-six camels;

one third-year camel for thirty-six camels;

one fourth-year camel for forty-six camels;

one fifth-year camel for sixty-one camels;

two third-year camels for seventy-six camels;

two fourth-year camels for ninety-one camels

for 120 camels or more, one must figure one three-year-old camel for every forty camels, or one four-year-old camel for every fifty camels, or calculate by brackets for fifty and forty, being very careful not to overlook any, and, if there are any left over, that the remainder be no more than nine. For example, if one owns 140 camels, he must give two four-year-old camels, for the first hundred and one three-year-old camel for the remaining forty. All camels given in payment of the *zakat* must be females.

Addenda

Shaving one's face, whether with bladed razors or electric apparatuses intended for the same purpose, is highly unacceptable.

❈ ❈ ❈ ❈

Beating of drums during athletic contests is not allowed; nor is the playing of military music during military ceremonies, if such music can in any way be assimilated to licentious music.

❈ ❈ ❈ ❈

Gambling is forbidden, even if indulged in not for gain but merely as an amusement.

❈ ❈ ❈ ❈

No Moslem is permitted to work in a Jewish concern, if he knows, or has the slightest suspicion, that this concern gives support to Israel. Money thus earned is impure.

* * * *

It is not strictly forbidden for Moslems to work for a concern managed by a Moslem which also employs Jews, provided the work does not serve Israel in any manner whatsoever. However, it is shameful to do one's work under the orders of a Jewish foreman.

* * * *

It is absolutely forbidden to dissect the corpse of a Moslem, but the dissection of non-Moslem corpses is permitted.

* * * *

The flesh of any animal slaughtered by the methods in use in various countries, where recently available machines are employed, is impure, and it is forbidden either to sell or to buy it. In such a transaction, the seller owes the buyer the money he paid for it, even if the animal was slaughtered while facing in the direction of Mecca, and even if the name of God was invoked at the time.

* * * *

Any meat imported from the countries of the infidels is strictly impure, and considered the same as the flesh of a corpse, unless it is proven that the cattle was slaughtered according to Moslem ritual.

✢ ✢ ✢ ✢

It is forbidden to look upon a woman other than one's wife, or an animal, or a statue, in a sensual or lubricious manner.

✢ ✢ ✢ ✢

A woman who wishes to pursue her studies toward the end of being able to earn her living through respectable work, and who has a male teacher, may do so if she keeps her face covered and has no contact with men; but if that is inevitable, and religious and moral tenets are thus undermined, she must give up her studies.

✢ ✢ ✢ ✢

Girls and boys who attend coeducational classes in grammar schools, high schools, universities, or other teaching establishments, and who, in order to legalize such a situation, wish to contract a temporary marriage may do so without the permission of their fathers. The same applies if the boy and girl are in love but hesitate to ask for such permission.

ABOUT THE EDITOR

TONY HENDRA is a freelance writer and editor, having collaborated on *The 80s: a Look Back* and *Not The New York Times*. He has written numerous articles for publications in America and France. Mr. Hendra holds a firstclass honors degee from Cambridge University in England.

ABOUT THE TRANSLATOR

HAROLD SALEMSON is a former journalist, film correspondent and film company executive. He has subtitled some two dozen foreign feature films in addition to translating over twenty books from French to English, including OUT by Pierre Rey.

ABOUT CLIVE IRVING

CLIVE IRVING's most recent book is *Crossroads of Civilization: 3,000 Years of Persian History*. He has worked as Managing Editor of the London Sunday *Times*, Consulting Editor to *McCalls* magazine and *New York* magazine, and head of Public Affairs at London Weekend Television. He is currently working on a special about Iran for *The David Frost Show*.